MW01242385

Ears
to
Hear

Suzan Jerome

All Scripture quotations, unless otherwise indicated, are taken from the New King James version of The Holy Bible, Reference Edition, © 1988 by Thomas Nelson, Inc., used with permission of the publisher.

Word Definitions used throughout come from The New Strong's Exhaustive Concordance of the Bible, Thomas Nelson Publishers, Nashville, 1990; or from The Expanded Vines Expository Dictionary of New Testament Words, Bethany House Publishers, Minneapolis, 1984; or from The New Wilson's Old Testament Word Studies, Kregel Publications, Grand Rapids, 1987, or from The New International Dictionary of New Testament Theology, Zondervan Publishing House, Grand Rapids, 1981.

To my brothers and sisters in the Lord, that we might move in peace through His school.

Contents

Foreword

There are some very strange sounds being heard in our society. They are not new sounds. They are merely variations on a theme written eons ago in the original battle between light and darkness. But these sounds seem louder, more penetrating, more devastating than in generations past because these sounds are hard to differentiate. There are the sounds of great choirs, singing forth the music of the masters, sung by musicians whose voices are trained to tuning fork precision, but whose ears are deaf to the angelic chorus.

There are the sounds of mighty, thundering preachers whose exegesis and exhortation are a match for St. Paul, but whose personal lives are warped by ambition, self-preservation and the fear of their personal fall from their pulpit pinnacle.

There are the sounds of the congregation, the people of God, the body of Christ. These are the strangest, most discordant sounds of all. These are the sounds of confusion, of conceit, of conservatism, and of carelessness. They are the sounds of lonely, helpless and confused believers banding together under a canopy of confusion. They seek "feeding" in a starving populace that cries out to be fed by them. They seek another "sign" as they stand in the blinding light of the risen Master. They listen for a "word" in the midst of their clanging symbols.

And I am no different, nor is the writer of this book. As long as any of us listens to the sounds of others we'll not be hearing the voice of the Father. The message of this book is simple: listen to God; get yourself into His environment and listen. But the message did not come easily to the author. There was a shaking of her foundations, a rattling of her bones, and many interruptions of her sleep, work, and personal goals before she finally

got the message. What you read herein is what she heard....
And is hearing.

I know Suzan Jerome in a limited way. I have been her teacher,
her advisor, her supervisor, and I hope, her friend. In all of the
above ways she has proven herself competent and caring. But
this book is about none of those areas of her—or my, or your—
competencies, except one: The willingness to listen to the Father.

The book is divided into four parts, each telling a portion of
one woman's spiritual journey. As you read, you will be struck
by several things. Some will puzzle you; some will make you
chuckle; some will bring a tear and cause you to reflect more
upon your own journey. But if you read carefully, and listen as
you read, you will hear a single question asked and answered:
"Who will be the Lord of your life?" If you come up with the
right answer, you will begin to hear new sounds, glorious
sounds, triumphant sounds. If you have ears to hear.

Larry Bjorklund

Preface

The Lord's preparation process for ministry can be rather mysterious, not like our process of required classes leading to a degree. In His process we might find ourselves in a number of positions that don't seem like the destination. Why is that? Because it is not about a degree; it is about a prepared heart. This little booklet tries to share what the fixed curriculum process looks like when united with the school the Lord runs Himself. You'll see what I mean as you read along.

I felt a call to ministry in 1979, having little idea what that would mean for my life. In 1981 I began working as an education director at a Methodist Church and as Assistant Minister a couple years later. Earlier I felt prompted to pursue more formal training, and enrolled in a Bible College, the only woman in their Christian Ministries master's program. A year and a half later I transferred to Fuller Seminary and started a Master of Divinity degree. I applied as a ministerial candidate in the Methodist Church and was accepted.

In the course of my first year of candidacy I found myself more and more involved in counseling people for faith crises or heart wounds or both. They needed a deeper connection with the Lord and access to His comfort to help with the crisis and enable them to face the heart wounds. In that process long-standing and unhealed emotional wounds were being uncovered. I began to feel "over my head" in unraveling the emotional blocks being revealed. It led me to enroll in yet another school where I ultimately earned a master's degree in marriage and family counseling. Larry Bjorklund was dean of that school, and I chose it largely because his teaching was what I had been looking for — someone who understood both the Lord's active involvement in the healing process and the realities of human brokenness.

Throughout these preparation avenues a recurring tension persisted. I often experienced an inability to integrate the principles presented in the training programs with my private experience of God working in my life. Nothing has been a greater struggle than to balance or understand the conflicting means of being prepared for ministry. Out of that struggle I have come to some imperfect understandings which this book seeks to share. Personal connection with the Lord was a central theme of Paul and the early disciples. Paul says he was called to preach the unsearchable riches of Christ to the Gentiles,

> *Eph. 3:9 and to make all see what is the fellowship of the mystery, which from the beginning of the ages has been hidden in God who created all things through Jesus Christ.*

I have long thought our best foundation is a deep, abiding connection with the Lord, to the point that He orders and directs our lives and we can hear Him well enough to let Him do so. Healing and purpose and empowering cannot fail to follow that foundation.

In my process of coming there myself, I discovered that there are two distinct paths involved in preparing believers for the work of ministry, one more visible and accessible than the other. There is the explicit and deliberate curriculum offered by various colleges and graduate programs. I sampled three forms of those schools and completed one program. The other is the school that God Himself runs; it begins with connection and proceeds to union. In fact, the whole point of His school is to restore us and teach us to live in active, vital, all-encompassing fellowship with Him, from which all ministry in His name flows.

The puzzling thing is He uses everything, the curriculum, our life in the church, our personal relationships, our family legacies, influence of husbands and wives, everything that happens to us is used in His school. So it isn't a matter of whether God sends us to the preparatory schools or not. I believe He often does. It isn't either/or. The issue is one of priority of the schools, and of the curriculum school realizing what that priority is. The way I have resolved the conflict is to put everything in my storehouse in the Lord's hands and place it at His disposal. It gives me peace to let Him select from the storehouse and prompt what to use and when; that saves me and others from counting on the limitations of my knowing.

Secondly, there is the difficulty for believers to see, distinguish, embrace God's school, run by His Holy Spirit. I believed it was mostly up to me to prepare myself for ministry. I was not able to believe that God Himself really does the preparation and knits it together in ways I would not conceive. It is only as I have let Him, made His school the priority, inch-by-inch giving it authority over the discordant or incomplete voices, that I have made personal progress.

Third, there is confusion in the church and from its teachings about whether we can actually hear from God. If we can, there is the question of what it will be like and how we can trust it. It is a formidable struggle to work through those questions, and the fact is God's school is tremendously personal, having its primary focus on the condition and motivation of our heart. For each person it is a private process, sprinkled with confusion, wonder, and concern about trusting their hearing of God. One of my professors in grad school said: "Suzan, don't you think it is dangerous to think you hear from God?" I found myself answering immediately: "Not as dangerous as not hearing from Him." Of course, some people just stop progress in His school and settle for the curriculum. That is a significant tragedy for the church. I do not believe that it will ever be easy for believers to make their way through this noisy mountain pass. It will always be full of fear and trembling. However, I do maintain that it is helpful to make both schools explicit and well-lighted.

I believe that is the purpose of this book. To state plainly that God has a personal school for each of us which we pursue with Him, in His time, by His provision, according to His purpose for us. There is no greater adventure than being rebuilt by Him. His school has priority because our primary life link is to Him, and in transforming the deepest regions of our heart into union with Him we will be preserved from contaminating the waters we serve in the name of the Lord Jesus Christ. I am sharing my own experience of what this amazing school has looked like in order to brighten the path leading into His school, hoping that those trying to find it will be assured of its existence and reliability.

The book begins in midstream. One of the characteristics of God's school is that it is difficult to determine when I entered or when I was not in His school.. What follows is a series of journal entries, taken from the year in which the Lord's school became explicit in my life.

Suzan Jerome

One

—— ⳟ ——

Serving in the Church

John 5:19,20 Then Jesus answered and said to them, "Most assuredly, I say to you, the Son can do nothing of Himself, but what He sees the Father do; for whatever He does, the Son also does in like manner. For the Father loves the Son, and shows Him all things that He Himself does, and he will show Him greater works than these, that you may marvel. .

John 5:44 How can you believe, who receive honor from one another, and do not seek the honor that comes from the only God?

Wednesday morning, 6-27-84

We are resuming the Wednesday morning group after two weeks off. Yesterday we began a new prayer time—at 2:00 at church. A number of people came. But we will have to see how that time works out. I have to say though that the prayer times of late have been amazing—filled with the Lord's presence and working by His own grace, not our directing which characterizes so much of our prayer—or has.

Tuesday morning, 7-3-84

The Lord is certainly bringing together understandings and setting me free from bondages I have operated in since I was a little girl. I read a description of part of the point, and I can relate to it directly because I have frequently felt that the response or expectation required of me was simply not in there to draw upon.

Anyway the statement in the Sandford's book (*Transformation of the Inner Man*) is: "More difficult to deal with than the negative experiences of our infancy is the lack of those positive experiences which should have brought us to life."

I noticed last night that I have been hurtful sometimes because of the trap I'm in in my own ability to love and receive love. I have been keen to help everyone instead of patient and humble in allowing God to pour out to me and use me in teaching His children at His own pace. And I have been striving somehow to satisfy an inner emptiness that I had no words for or real understanding of, but which is the source of the hurt I sometimes inflict on others.

I have everything to learn about how little I know and how ill-equipped I am to be directing others. I can only be a part of what the Lord is seeking to do by being a vessel through which His hand becomes visible. But first I must receive wholeness myself, turning over those deep heart fears and insecurities that I have struggled to hide and deny and proceed past until they are healed. Until the empty places are filled, I have no wholeness to share. Hard to look at but true.

Monday morning, 7-9-84

The Sunday evening service began last night. It was wonderful, Lord—the strong, faithful sense of Your presence, our praise lifted up and You touching and ministering and calling out Your children. I don't remember any time of nervousness, but there was something going on that made me very tired by the time I got home. When I got to bed, the Lord showed me about it. The tiredness was from holding the door open against all the weight on it to close—a kind of wave upon wave of buffeting to close off the promise of the Lord which He by His presence witnessed to our spirits, causing us to understand more than we have words to describe.

Wednesday morning, 7-11-84

I had in mind a day off today—at least the whole morning through lunch, but it turns out I am meeting with someone this morning and having lunch with someone else. Lord, I'm sure feeling too little today. A heaviness abounds over all the tearing and falling apart everywhere. The prime examples in our church of marriage and leadership are on the brink of divorce. A dear brother is going blind and not letting anyone in on it. Another is ready to leave the church, holding on by a thread, "string" as he put it yesterday.

Lord, we need some miracles. We need such an evidence of Your presence and power. Actually, we always need that. Why isn't it happening more, Lord?

> Because you won't humble yourselves to receive.

How do we need to humble ourselves, Lord? What shall we do?

> Pray. Seek your answers in prayer.

What are we doing instead?

> Trying to get what you think you want to happen.

How can we hear that, Lord?

> By breaking; by the falling apart of your efforts.

What are You doing in this church these days?

> Allowing you to reap what you sow.

We don't know that, Lord, and can't see it. Have mercy on us, Lord.

> You begin to see it; teach them; tell them. That is why
> I have shown you.

Thursday night, 7-12-84

Early this evening I began to respond to a sense I had much of the day, to get quiet before the Lord. So I went over to church with the intention of spending some time in the sanctuary. As it turned out when I got there, I went into the chapel instead—because the issue was somehow related to the last time I went to the chapel to pray. The day of the conference (Signs and Wonders) when they talked about spiritual gifts, tongues in particular, and I realized my failure to receive was related to my own resistance. Something inside me would not let me.

Tonight I went to pray about Sunday evening and the closing prayer time that is shaping up. But I never got to that issue. The point the Lord raised was this business of experiencing things in our spirit while we were still in the womb. I was reminded that my mom didn't want me—didn't want me the whole time she was carrying me, not until I was born and had brown hair and brown eyes. Then she was delighted because she had always wanted a girl who looked like her. It was as though I experienced not being welcome in the womb that carried me, and it was so overwhelmingly sad. It seemed to have everything to do with the difficulty I have had feeling that I belong. I really never have felt that fully. And I could see why—if I didn't "belong" or wasn't welcome in the womb, where would I be? That was the argument my heart presented to the Lord. But the Lord showed me He was present; I could sense His outstretched hands receiving me at birth. It was His plan, and His welcome began to overrule my mom's perspective.

But I also saw my lifetime of efforts to disprove that by being worthy, doing good, doing things that pleased others—a frantic effort to cover, justify and so nullify that undeniable truth of being unwelcome. It was a challenge to receive His welcome in exchange because looking at unwelcome is so painful we have to be rebuilt enough to have the strength to go there.

The Lord worked through forgiveness of my mom with me. She, of course, had no way of knowing how that would impact me.

We worked through forgiving of myself for the judgments and concealed anger it produced. But I couldn't seem to get over not being wanted. Then the Lord gave me a series of Scriptures I had never quite seen in this light.

> *John 1:12 But as many as received Him, to them He gave the right to become children of God, to those who believe in His name.*

I could see that I was God's child and had been foreseen and provided for. Then as I sat there with my eyes closed, I saw a little light ball. A fetus in the midst of utter darkness and the Scripture came to mind,

> *John 1:4 In Him was life, and the life was the light of men.*

The Lord showed me that I was never unwelcome to Him. He had planned for me, knew me before the foundation of the world. And He *said* to me: "You were never unwelcome to Me."

Then I was given a Scripture which I had to look up and found in Ps. 110:3

> *Your people shall be volunteers in the day of Your power, In the beauties of holiness, from the womb of the morning, You have the dew of Your youth*

A profound healing was taking place. It will change everything about me. I won't have to strive to belong, constantly defending myself; I can now accept and choose to be healed, rather than continue in combat.

Thursday morning, 7-19-84

I have a new insight about the word "approve" in Phil 1:10. The definition says it has two meanings: To stand up on, to rise up against. They seem to be contradictory — standing up on is a positive action; rising up against a negative action. The reason both meanings are true at once is because it is inevitable that if we stand up on something, we are also rising up against something else—in choosing there is excluding of other things. It's like the word for repentance—reconsidering and therefore turning. When you turn toward God, you inevitably turn away from other things.

This might explain why human beings kind of like confusion. So long as we are confused, we cannot stand up on anything surely, and so don't have to rise up against anything or make any definite statement about what is "excellent" (and what is not excellent). So we are all reticent to stand up on with conviction, which should teach us to stand up only on what God says. But it doesn't; it teaches us not to stand up at all, to be reticent to approve what is excellent, to hedge..

I don't know how I am going to share this, Lord.

Friday evening, 7-27-84

I'm tired tonight, Lord, and I need some understanding of the tiredness that comes along after a day of fullness. Do I expend more of my own energy than I need to?

> You get excited and gathered up in the individual things I am doing and perform My word in an agitated state. You could rest quietly in My peace and use less energy—leaving more for the quiet times with Me, like now.

Hmm. How do I do that, Lord.

> Focus on Me instead of so intently on what we are doing at the moment.

The answer came as I began to write the question—almost before I finished forming it in my mind. I've been reminded so much lately of the supernatural, power of God moments that have happened in my life and for a long time. I've considered them isolated instances and not thought about them as being a usual way of life. But more and more I look toward that day.

Today P. said she didn't feel good and was going home a little early. I said to her, "Okay, go ahead; I'll be here until closing, get some good sleep." The Lord said to me: "Pray for her before she goes." So I asked P. if I could pray for her. She laughed and said, "Sure." I put my hands on her shoulder near her neck. They were only there briefly when she said, "Your hands are so hot." I half apologized, though I was unaware of it really. Anyway, her headache went away and she said there was no need to go home and didn't. God is beginning to answer the prayer about healing. Hallelujah!

I say that, but at the same time I know it's going to be a progressive battle, getting more difficult as we proceed. But that's okay. What I notice is that when God says pray for something, He does something about it. That's the important key!

Wednesday morning, 8-1-84

I went to the evangelism work area meeting last night. I had an idea that it was an important meeting. But I didn't realize why. It turned out to be important for clarifying things, not because of the programming ahead. At the end of the meeting B. said we have to ask the Lord what he wants us to do. I was disheartened and tired, but my heart did ask the question and agreed that we needed to do that. The answer came clearly and quickly:

Quit propping it up.

There is some kind of breaking of will at hand. The people I have cared for are in jeopardy of being broken in spirit unless it brings them to a glorious liberty in the presence of the Lord, notwithstanding the circumstances. That is my job, I am convinced—to be one of the Lord's tools for presiding over the denial and death of self we must go through before we are useful.

I have been standing alongside many while God performs that in all of our lives. He has had to work it in my life over and over to enable me to persist in the situations and weather the storms. What a time it has been.

Wednesday evening, 8-1-84

I see, however dimly, that too much emphasis has been on this church and the people here and not enough directly on the Lord. I am riddled with more emotions than I can identify today. A real sorrow over the cost and the resistance and loss. A real amazement at the Lord's faithfulness to bring about His will. A growing sense of call to do something about the plight of church leaders — pastors in particular. I continue to believe that I am unqualified and unable to do anything about it. Yet, I continue to have the call confirmed.

I've been expecting some major change. But the only thing I hear is that I need to keep doing what I was told until His children are out of the wilderness. What's the wilderness, Lord?

> The place of proving, testing, learning the fear of the Lord.

What does it look like when we get out?

> Seeking My face with all your heart. You are to shepherd the children I have brought to you until they and you learn to seek Me with your whole heart.

Tuesday afternoon, 8-7-84

Today I was just in a funny place. When I went to church today, it was almost as though I had no place there and nothing to do. I don't know what's happening, but I would say that I am coming upon a choice point of some kind. I don't know what will happen to bring it into focus, but I feel as though I am being prepared for another direction. I have never been able to feel like I will be led into the office of pastor of a church. I can't really feel that coming together though I am in a program that leads there presumably. I am going over to the church for a prayer time. There will be other people there from the seminar. I don't know what I need to pray about, but I know I need to be in prayer.

Tuesday evening, 8-7-84

Well, no one but C. showed for the prayer group. I am having a hard time with Your church today, Lord. Your children come and go as they choose, leaving whatever they leave.

I have been in a heavy place recently — the last couple of days. This morning I have a new view of the territory that the Lord gave me as I sat down to pray. He's burning up, clearing away, separating out the wood, hay and stubble. No process is more painful, and I guess my job is to go round encouraging and loving everyone who is participating in that pruning time so they don't inadvertently give away any gold with the clearing of lesser things. It's hard to see sometimes.

It is another word very like the one I received after the evangelism meeting — Quit propping it up. Another thing I heard this morning — we've been asking God to come and do what He wants with this church. Well, He's come and He's carrying out the filthiness (2 *Chron. 29:5*), making it impossible for it to stand. So the question becomes, "What can stand?"

Well, praise and worship can, counting on Him instead of each other can. It doesn't look like much else can today. Of course that simplifies the issues marvelously. If we could just stand up on them and rise up against the others, the progression would turn to joy and thanksgiving.

Thank You, Lord for the light I am receiving as I go along.

Saturday evening, 8-11-84

I was aware when I went to Wrightwood this summer for a weekend retreat alone that a new dimension in my relationship with the Lord, and probably with others, was at hand. My view of God began to change there. It changed more, and those Wrightwood changes were confirmed at the Signs and Wonders Conference. Despite my intentional low profile I am nevertheless establishing wider contacts and being included in a wider sphere of involvement. I am heading for some kind of teaching/preaching ministry within the church that has a specific thrust and is perhaps aimed at leaders — pastors and others.

What is the topic or thrust or teaching?

Healing

Healing? That is certainly not what I would have put down if I were figuring it out. Lord, how does healing apply to pastors/leaders?

They all must be healed before they can be tools for My healing of My children. They are broken in the first place, as you all are, and then further broken by the impossible weight of bringing healing to others outside of complete dependence on Me and receiving first what they are to give.

Have I received Your healing, Lord? Am I in any way qualified by that definition?

You are receiving. You'll remember Me telling you that you came to southern California to be healed. I've been working that.

Lord, I don't see myself as one who has healing gifts. Do I?

You could see and feel them flowing at the conference and felt in your heart a call to healing.

Yes, I remember that. But I thought it was probably me. Why healing, Lord?

> It's dear to My heart and the foundational need of all of My sheep—especially My shepherds.

How am I going to be able to talk to them, Lord?

> I will make the door and open it.

Two

———— ✂ ————

Returning

Sunday night, 8-12-84

M. and I went to the Vineyard tonight. The message was from
Ps. 145—about praise being spoken, shared, proclaimed daily.
During the ministry time I felt the Lord prompting me to come
daily to the sanctuary as I used to—to commune with Him daily
and take all my direction and priority from Him. I've drifted
from that place of communication. John Wimber talked about
losing the romance of the early days. He's said that before and
I've paid no attention, thinking that I was already there, and
to some degree I was. But I have lost that marvelous friend-
ship quality my days held when I talked with the Lord about
everything and longed for the times of apartness to hear from
Him. Now I move rapidly through the days, producing less
fruit, or at least feeling less praise and joy. That's a danger sign
of the first order, and it's time for me to return. I've heard the
same message I heard tonight a number of times, but I haven't
obeyed it fully. Am I deceived, Lord or stubborn?

   You are the first because you are the second.

So You really are saying, "come daily to the physical building of
the sanctuary and be with Me?"

   Daily.

Monday morning, 8-13-84

It is true, Lord, that I have lost some of the closeness of contact and communication I once had. I have gotten so involved in doing Your work and/or ministering to Your children that I do not have time left for You, and I have grown impatient with being still and listening — too much to "do."

I have also gotten depleted and tired and feel little joy in the work — whether it is church or school. I have a sense of being driven through a prescribed set of activities. It certainly seems time for a new or restored priority. I recall as I have many times how I came and talked with You daily when I first took this job. I scheduled my whole day around talking to You. And during that time I heard all the things I needed to for the day and the events at hand. I came away equipped in some bright and comforting way.

Now I must be running on memory, or on the moments of revelation You give me for others. The closest I get to reading your word for myself is some aspects of the Sunday evening preparation. And a week or so ago when I was looking for Scriptures on comfort, I felt so desperately in need of it.

So here I am, Lord, acknowledging that things have gotten empty. I am embarrassed and ashamed to have left You in some sense. Worse than that You have told me about it quietly a number of times, for longer than I care to face — from the time I ceased going to the sanctuary daily. That was over a year ago.

It seems I am at a point where nothing will do except talking to You — nothing I can write, or say; the only thing now is a fresh word and experience of being in the presence of and in communion with my Father. Nothing is the same, nothing is a good substitute, nothing produces the same outcome. So I will go to the sanctuary today.

Tuesday morning, 8-14-84

I am tired of all the substitutes and "about God" things, tired of all the wheels spinning in the sand simulating movement, or sounding like it at least. I will be surprised if there is any-one at the prayer group this afternoon. Most of the members are gone to Ashram or on vacation. But whether anyone comes or not I am going to spend time in the sanctuary, part of my process of returning to a relationship and communion I should never have left. I would not be in this tired, discouraged place if I had stayed. And this kind of pit I don't seem to pop out of; I have to walk back down the trail to the clearing I left. I have to walk out. The habit of mind, sensitivity of hearing, consistent turning to and asking, setting aside time for no other purpose than to be with God; they have all been weakened. They are the means for holding communion in place; now they have to be reestablished. What I have done instead is get all caught up in circumstances, moving into them with the thought of doing something about them. But all I really did was move away from the wherewithal to do something about them — if they are even the point. I have been learning to see circumstances and people instead of learning to see God. And I have gotten very tired.

I read about the call of Moses last night — all of his excuses for not going. I could see all of mine in them, but then I read the point where he said, in effect, Lord, send someone else. I felt an overwhelming pain and deep sadness in my chest.

My sense of calling comes from when You said, "The Church of My Spirit is deserted and locked." The church run by Your Spir-it became deserted. How did that happen? And it says that after it was left empty, it was locked so we cannot get back in. How did that happen? Probably by the kind of drifting from which I am now recovering.

I believe the church of His Spirit became deserted when the power of God ceased to attest to the work of the church because it was more our work than His. Then a rationale for that change locked the doors and we have not been able to cut through and find our way back. The church of His Spirit has taken a beating ever since. Now there is a tremendous move of the Holy Spirit and a gradual rediscovery of the principle Jesus laid down so simply and definitely: "I only do what I see the Father doing."

Well, what do I see You doing today, Lord. We have to start somewhere.

Tuesday afternoon, 8-14-84

Well, Lord, it seems the consensus of opinion is that there is an effort at hand to get rid of me.[1] Most of my life that would have hurt

---

1   It was primarily the pastor who wanted me to go. I first served under a charismatic pastor and his wife who were open to the Holy Spirit. Several charter members of the church were offended by the new direction and style of ministry, though the church was growing tremendously. They complained to the District Superintendent vociferously and succeeded in getting the pastor moved and a new pastor appointed. He and I were not on the same page. I thought I would, of course, go and let him have the kind of Assistant Minister he wanted. But the Lord said, "you are staying." It seemed so inappropriate for me to stay that I asked how that could be. He said, "you have invited people out into the stream and you will see them across." That was true, lots of people were in groups and/or individual prayer, and I was shepherding them through a healing process. I was also told to stay by the District Superintendent for continuity. At one point, I was asked to report my hours, which I did for about three weeks; then I was asked to stop reporting them because it became evident to all of us that I was working twice as many hours as I was being paid for. That tension, and continuing ministry, went on for a year and a half. I was well received by the congregation, and loved by many of the people I ministered to directly. When the Lord finally said, "Now it is time to go," I let the pastor know that I would be resigning. His question was, "Will you be leaving the church as well?" It was an odd position to be in, though a perfect storm for personal refining.

my feelings. Now I just want to know, What do You say, Lord? Is it true? Is it going to work? What shall I do in the face of it?

> Love them.

Are there attitudes and motivations that can be used to cause division and get in the way of what You would do with this time? What are they?

> Still some old hurts over people in authority who let you down.

> Lack of expectation that they will ever do any better and so failure to encourage them to be all they can be—as you encourage others who are not upholding pride of office or position.

> Still some personal separation—lack of a sense of being in it together which results in a false martyrdom, or poor Suzan, having to absorb all this struggle.

What must I do, Lord?

> Forgive your parents, the teachers who didn't live up to being teachers, leaders everywhere who did not meet needs that really should have been met long before—needs that only I can meet now. The need to be significant, to belong, to be loved for yourself alone. I provide all of that.

If I really believe that, Lord, what will it enable me to do?

> You would be able to minister to leaders as you minister to those who can more humbly receive. You would be able to go over to them without judgment or guilt over how you sometimes view them.

Thursday morning, 8-15-84

Yesterday in prayer one of the topics was my family. I saw several specific issues calling for forgiveness, and walked through them slowly with the Lord. Then somehow we went from forgiving them to me being forgiven. Oh, yes, I thought; He was asking me if I have received forgiveness for my choices. I could see that I had kind of blamed the church, my family and found a lot of justifications for leaving the Lord when I was a teenager. But I had never simply and plainly acknowledged that it was my choice, stemming from my own heart; so I confessed to the Lord that I chose other things instead of Him. It caused a break in our relationship, and I've never just come and honestly said that's what happened. I'm not pleading any extenuating circumstances anymore. I chose, I did it, and I need Your forgiveness.

I saw that there was a core root of guilt and defensiveness. The response of the Lord is the most amazing thing I have ever "seen." It was not the response of the Holy Spirit; it was Father God. I was sitting on the back porch praying when I said that to Him. I was kind of swept into His presence, at what point, or by whom I don't know, but there I was, aware of a great rejoicing and jubilation. There was a tremendous celebration with singing and dancing, multiple instruments and an amazing outpouring of love. Then I was being decked in a finely woven, light and flowing robe of gold, woven I knew by the work and blood of Jesus. I found myself saying: "Finally, I am loved. Finally, I am loved."

What I see as a result of it is that I've never clearly identified and confessed the root sin of my life—that of choosing anyone or anything over God. It is the very nature of sin. It is amazing to me what a simple process it was and how enormous the sense of release. It's an acknowledging of the truth; we've chosen things and people over God, and then asking forgiveness as He reveals the tremendous cost in life and love. It is so simple. But the process of coming to that realization is anything but simple.

All these years I have been struggling and lurching toward this place. This morning I came to the threshold and was welcomed in. Praise God!

I could see the love and patience and faithfulness of the Father — gently leading me, patiently revealing line upon line, causing my heart to inquire and then answering my inquiry with more of Him. Several Scriptures were quickened to me. Especially the one where Paul says he is the least of the apostles because he persecuted the church: But by the grace of God I am what I am. That is now the only thing I have to say, by the grace of God I am what I am. The robe He gave me is gorgeous, and in the Father's eyes so am I.

I was not able to see and receive this depth of acceptance and love when I first chose the Lord. But He is so full of love and mercy that He takes whatever part of the whole work that is available and starts there. He's willing to start wherever we can.

Saturday morning, 8-18-84

It's a quiet morning and still cool. I'm sitting on the back porch with my tea.

When I was sitting in the chapel yesterday and selecting songs for Sunday morning, I asked the Lord why I felt a kind of weariness with the task — almost boredom. I believe the answer was that we are perpetually feeding ourselves. We are not taking what we have and giving it to those who don't have, perpetually feeding ourselves and occupied with whether we are well fed or not. I'm bored with it, and it is pointless after a while. There is only a certain degree of growth you can come to without reaching out, which is itself further growth and one that cannot be accomplished in any other way. I think there is even a way in which we cease to receive until we give away what we just got.

I am in that position. I have opportunity to give away all I have received, and I seem never to receive from the Lord without a soon opportunity turning up to give to someone else. But my giving is to believers, not unbelievers. So I have a bunch of half-grown children of God around me and am half-grown myself.

I saw, too, on Thursday morning that the ax gets applied more to the branches than to the root of the tree. That means we are perpetually just keeping up with cutting off the same things, and are subject to manifold outpouring of condemnation while seeking to cut off the branches of sin, while the root continues to produce them. It's very hard on our faith. So why don't we just go ahead and cut the root, bring down the whole tree? For one thing it is scary to take so drastic a step. For another it appears radical to everyone we know and love, and we cannot risk losing approval/regard. And finally, we do not know clearly what the root is — not sharply enough to locate and sever it.

Saturday evening, 8-18-84

This has been an amazing day. More has happened than I can write down. I never can write down what God does and shows me. But I need to say enough to have a reminder and make a record. Sometimes I wonder why.

This afternoon I went for a walk and thought through the teaching I am receiving and will give tomorrow night. Then I just asked the Lord to talk to me. I wanted to just walk along and talk to Him, or listen really. He said how glad He was that I had come and how He delights to have His children come before Him and walk in His presence. That is what I would be doing for the rest of my life. He said we would go many places together and win many victories in the world, restoring hearts and fulfilling His word. He said I would greatly exalt Him, which made me cry touching, joyful tears.

When I got home, I decided to go for an ice cream cone. As I was eating it, the day seemed so beautiful and the tape I was listening to so lovely, that I kept driving along praising the Lord. I was well down Orange Avenue and realized I was only a block or so from where I turn to go to Forest Lawn where my dad is buried. It instantly occurred to me to drive over there. It seemed kind of peculiar until I began to link the visit with the forgiveness session of Thursday morning. So I figured I was going over to establish it somehow, and so I was.

Standing there at his grave I began to think of where he is now, how sorry he probably was that he didn't know when he was here what he knows now and wishing he could say. By some kind of grace of the Lord I received an apology of my father. I understood that once free he would wish he'd been able to give more of himself, wish he had not been too prideful to know the Lord in humility, that he had been able to join me more in knowing Him. There was also a sense that being both aware, there would be a long time to share the understanding when I was on the other side, too. I'd say it was a time of my earthly father asking forgiveness and seeking to deliver blessing. As I stood there I remembered the hug he gave me the day I was married. He had tears in his eyes and said: "Have a beautiful life." So he did desire to give me his blessing. Standing there at his grave we were in the Lord together, forgiving each other for missed opportunities and looking forward to the time of praising God in eternity.

Then I was ready to go along and finish what remains of my walk here, with the sense that he was glad I had found the Lord, I was aware of his blessing and that a mutual forgiveness was in place. It was amazing! I felt closer to my father than I ever did when he was living. I felt we were mysteriously together in it. It was quite a gift.

Monday morning, 8-20-84

I need to go to work soon. I have been up a long time, did some pruning, put out the trash, have the water going on the front yard. I have even written a letter and have it ready to mail.

I am aware of an indescribable presence of the Lord these days. I knew that the experience Thursday morning was one of the most significant of my life. Since then I have felt a kind of wave of love and compassion and tenderness for a lot of people and a wholly new love for the Lord. It warms and softens the days, and I have noticed a growing ease of hearing correction and curbing in certain areas. The things the Lord is revealing in His word have also sharpened. I have had a new joy, even in the face of the heaviness around me, especially in our church.

Tuesday morning, 8-21-84

This morning I got up still troubled over the meeting at church the night before. I realized I was not looking at the Lord. I was looking again at all the mess and dim prospects for the life of the Spirit in this church now. I am seeing, being shown that I absolutely must keep my eyes on Jesus, none of these situations are tolerable otherwise, and they would cause me to quit and go if the effort coming from wings of discouragement had its way. But I will learn to keep my eyes on Jesus. I can no longer live anywhere else. I got a view this morning of the power that bestows, and that is what I want. I want to be a vessel through which God moves in power, but I could see that I cannot be that while I keep getting caught up in circumstances and use them as logic with which to plot the future. The future is not for me to decide; it is something my mind automatically churns out unless it is caught up and refocused on the Lord continually.

This is something I must do. I must take dominion over my mind and charge it to look at the Lord for all of its directives and interpretations and guidance. Paul says: The weapons of our warfare are not carnal, but mighty through God to the pulling down of strong holds; casting down imaginations, and every high thing that exalts itself against the knowledge of God and bringing into captivity every thought to the obedience of Christ (2 Cor. 10:4,5). What I am wrestling with today is what that looks like being taken hold of and lived in! I begin to see that the means of learning it are to experience over and over what happens when we do not bring our thoughts into captivity and obedience. That scattering that occurs when we are led into and through circumstances and tossed around by them instead of continually asking, "Lord, what do You say about this?"

Tuesday night, 8-21-84

We had an amazing administrative council meeting tonight. It flowed right along. This afternoon we had a prayer group, and this evening I spent the hour before the meeting in praise and prayer. I have begun to pray when I feel called to prayer, and as I come, I ask the Holy Spirit to guide me in prayer. Tonight I asked that, and as I knelt down and closed my eyes the words that came were:

> In the name of the Lord Jesus Christ, stop it!

It really stunned me, and I was saying them in my under-standing several times before I recognized that they *were* my guidance in prayer. I asked for clarification and felt that I was to speak that in my spirit to everything that happened or be-gan to happen that was not of the Lord. That was my only job at the meeting — to stand in prayer. So the rest of the time I spent in praise and fellowship. I had asked for direction about what to say at the point on the agenda where it says: Assistant to the Minister. I didn't get any response, and sure enough when we got there, the only thing to say was "praise God for this meeting."

I'm reminded of the Scripture about letting everything you say be only for edifying the other. That would eliminate a certain amount of what I say.

> *Eph. 4:29 Let no corrupt word proceed out of your mouth, but what is good for necessary edification, that it may im-part grace to the hearers.*

It is followed by "Do not grieve the Holy Spirit of God" — the link is obvious.

I have been noticing something this last week or so. Prayer is tremendously effective. God is willing to guide us in it, reveal His will and lead us to pray for it, but it takes a lot of time to see one major prayer request through to an end. I see that it has to be focused, deep, persistent prayer until we pray through it.

It's almost 11:00, and I am tired, but I know any number of issues that need prayer and require the focused prayer I was just talking about. Lord, we need more pray-ers, more laborers.

Tomorrow I have a day off and a new journal to start. The Scriptures that herald it are *2 Cor. 10:4,5* and *Eph. 4:29,30*. It might be one of the most momentous steps to date because it looks like we've arrived at the taming of the tongue stage. I am no longer going to be able to give free rein to what I think. I have been hearing that for a while. When I get to a solid view of the damage I have done, I hope You have a good hold of me, Lord. I've been verbal for so long. Nevertheless, I am excited about the prospect. It will grow me up and make me more trustworthy and gracious. It's high time. It's time for me to stop indulging myself. I agree with You in producing and establishing that, Lord. It might take the rest of my life, but let's do it!

Wednesday night, 8-22-84

I went for a drive and ended up at a mid-week worship service in Cerritos, friends of D. They are neat people. He was preaching on yielding ourselves to God. It certainly struck a chord for me. I am obedient when I hear God, but I could not say that I am really yielded—whole heartedly. Anyway, I went to the altar, and two people prayed for me at different times. I felt the Holy Spirit come upon me, and I know I was praying for a yielded heart. I believe I heard the Lord say that He would give me a yielded heart. I could see tonight that it isn't, but I could not see what about it is not yielded. I could just feel that it wasn't. I heard the word, and I went to the altar and asked. God said He would do it. No telling what is in store for me in order for him to answer that prayer. I think that yieldedness requires real breaking.

Lord, there is something about me that is not simple and open and yielded. What is it? What are they?

> Your reputation isn't yielded.

What do I have to do to yield it?

> Lose it.

What is my reputation?

> Smart, together, can do anything.

How do I lose it, Lord?

> I'll take care of that.

What else do I need to yield?

> Your security financially

You'll take care of that, too?

Why were You bringing up that issue tonight?

> Preparation/warning

Monday morning, 9-3-84

I was looking again, briefly, at the series we have launched on Sunday night. It's an amazing series, Lord. The actual truth about who we are in Christ is astounding. We have been deceived and robbed of our household, left with a bunch of furniture.

This morning I got up with a new perspective. It's not one that has been settled upon or analyzed in words, but perhaps I can say something about it—I know it is part of the process of being "renewed in the spirit of your mind." The change is hard to describe, but it has to do with expectation. I have always been looking for a place where everything is in order and where I have rounded some final bend in the road and reached the top of the mountain. That is the "spirit of my mind." I do not have the attitude of serving and being a part of building the habitation of God which is constantly being added to, certain of the eventual outcome, building in faith, working and rejoicing in the process. Unless we are renewed in that spirit of our minds, we'll always be in tension with what God is doing — a thousand generations is a while (*Deut 7:9*). That is a completely different attitude of mind, but with it no single situation is the final word. It is not the expectation I had in mind, but it is more real and livable. I'll be spending the rest of my life learning to live out *Eph. 4:12-15*.

Wednesday morning, 9-5-84

A question still remains about applying for ordination next June. There was a time when I thought the Lord was saying to apply for ordination. But I wonder if He doesn't have a different view of ordination than the Methodist Church has. For one thing He thinks He has already ordained me, and so do I. When I took this job on staff, He said He had ordained me for it, and as I recall he said that men would get around to it. I'm not sure what that means or how it looks and the question and underlying discomfort remain. I'll have to see how he settles it in my heart.

I have the strangest mixture of things going on in me these days. On the one hand, I realize that the situation at church is really at a crisis point and it cannot continue without some change in the near future. But on the other hand, I seem to be nearer to a place of praising God independently of the circumstances than I have ever been or seriously entertained. It is as though praise and fellowship and the opening of his word to me are so evident and growing that it really doesn't matter about the circumstances. I don't think I have ever really gotten a view of this place before.

What an amazing time for it to happen—when the situation at this church is at an all-time low, and when it is 100 degrees outside and no sign of it breaking. That's amazing, Lord!

Tuesday morning, 9-11-84

This morning is dramatically different from the preceding days. I've been running from one thing to the next, and at each point was intercepted by someone in real personal crisis. But this morning I have no schedule for a couple of hours, it's cooler, praise the Lord, and raining. I'm sitting here on the back porch with time to read and write and pray. The Scripture that occurred to me was from *Hebrews 10:36*: you have need of patience that after you have done the will of God, you may receive the promise.

I don't know what has been happening to me lately, but I believe it stems from a series of prayers I prayed about "seeing" the Lord, drawing nearer, not being tossed and swayed by circumstances. The Lord is answering that prayer. I have felt a patience and constancy of faith in the midst of the difficult days of trial all around. And here this morning is an outpouring of blessing. The spiritual nature of the battle begins to be more apparent, and with it comes a basis on which to reject some things and stand waiting on the Lord for real truth.

There's a dove up in the avocado tree saying some loud "who-who's." It's a quiet, soft rain, hasn't apparently poured because some things are not wet yet. It's one of the soft, soaking kind—exactly what we need, and I am thanking You, Lord. I'm grateful both for the blessing of this morning and for the testing and proving and new ground emerging from the difficulties.

There's been a change in me in the last few weeks, hasn't there, Lord? I guess it has been happening since the week before the Signs and Wonders Conference, with the weekend in Wrightwood. What an amazing time that was, and I see the fruit of it appearing now and to come. You bless me greatly, Father; I love

You. I'm closer to living in a place of praise instead of visiting it sporadically. That is what I wanted, and you are answering. That must mean it was what You wanted first.

Wednesday morning, 9-12-84

Lord, I'm feeling incomplete somehow this morning. Before long I'm going over to the hospital to see B., and I sense that I am very partially equipped to minister to her. I believe Your healing power is available to your children, but I have not become a regular vessel for it. And so I am going to see her with less than I could bring if I were the more consistent channel I want to be. I believe that is a great deal of my uneasiness this morning.

I'm feeling undermined or something. You tell me what I am feeling.

> Some of it is flak, designed to cripple you when you do get there. If you believe you are ineffective, you will be.

What's the rest, the part Your Spirit is author of?

> Calling you up higher.

In what way, Lord?

> Risking with others, not caring what it looks like.

How does that relate to going this morning?

> Hospitals are intimidating. It's hard to maintain the sovereignty of God in them. It's hard to even talk about it because everyone there seems to deny its power. There is not an influence or atmosphere of faith. You have to bring it and keep it.

What shall I do this morning, Lord when we go?

> Push back the darkness by command in My name. Praise Me as you walk along; don't forget that each step is a spiritual battle in which you are taking a land that belongs to the enemy — wrenching it away on My authority. Don't shrink before the darkness or in any way agree with its power.

Lord, what do You want to do with B? She's fairly new to the church, at a time when things are crazy.

> Release her from trusting anything other than Me. Send My word to heal her.

A word I can bring from Your Scripture?

> *John 10*

Thursday night, 9-13-84

Tomorrow is Friday, and that means up early for the prayer group, and we're starting at 6:30 instead of 7:00. This weekend is going to be a full one, but at least someone else is responsible for the situation. In that sense I have the evening off Sunday, though I am going.

Anyway, regardless of the weekend, the busyness, the degree and amount of trial going on, I nonetheless have a new place of fellowship with God. It's a place from which He can convict me more easily, forgive me more thoroughly, and where I can love Him more freely than ever before. It's wonderful!

Friday afternoon, 9-14-84

Something very unusual is happening to me, and I can't tell yet whether it blesses or concerns me. I have gone around for several days with such an intense feeling of love for people. The only thing I can compare it to in intensity is when I prayed to be filled with the Holy Spirit and a few weeks later had the experience I called baptism. From then on I had a physical feeling of overflowing, as though I were in a warm bath slightly charged with electricity. It happened every time I talked to the Lord, asked Him questions, felt led to do something. When I first experienced it, I thought, am I going to go around the rest of my life like this?! I thought I had someone with me all the time, when they hadn't been before, and it was so unusual I had some mixed feelings about that, too.

That's how I feel about this feeling of loving people. For one thing, it hurts. I feel like saying something loving to them all the time because I'm aware of their pain. I have a combined sense of longing on their behalf, prayer and love that really is peculiar.

When I asked the Lord why I was feeling that way, I believe He said it was how He feels about His children, and I remembered the Scripture He gave me about having many more children than a married woman. I guess it's true.

Anyway, it seems that the feeling of loving others has come, and it is an actual physical response which I have only ever experienced in fleeting moments, but now is hanging around for days. What has happened, Lord?

> You gave up what you were doing instead, and that's what I replaced it with—My love for My children. Aren't they beautiful? And it is my greatest gift—my gift of love and the freedom to love. I bless and honor you, as you do Me. I delight to give that gift above all others. It is a culmination of My work in a life. God is love.

I know I will get used to it, Lord, like I got used to the electrical stirring and witness of Your Spirit within. This is almost as amazing as that was. It has come on the heels of loving you more, of walking through the days in love with Jesus. I know that sounds peculiar to a lot of people. It sounds a little peculiar to me, but it sure is beautiful. Thank You, Father!

Tuesday morning, 9-18-84

Well, it's really been an uphill couple of days, walking through the aftermath of Sunday night and the growth points of people in dealing with it. And now there is the preparation for tonight's meeting at which it will be discussed.

BUT this morning brought a piece of news that overshadows it all! The word from B. is that God has healed her. The doctors say they don't understand it; she had cancer and now the results of the biopsy are that she doesn't have it. I just found out this morning. I forgot to call her yesterday when the results were supposed to get back. I was so involved in all of the church affairs, and that's also a lesson to me because I got so caught up in it that I probably also forgot that God is a healing, loving God and that is what He is bringing about.

Saturday morning, 9-25-84

I found myself describing my role today. It's the role of spiritual mom or discipler, or mentor, or whatever you call it, but it's going along with someone until they are themselves solidly established in their relationship with the Lord and can stand on their hearing and worship and praise and discernment. It takes a while and has to be carried out in intimate relationship in which some real heart feelings, hurts, dreams, trauma and disappointments are shared. I could see that today; it's happened too much to miss. I could also see that I was the wedge to break loose the central issues in lives that need healing, are in the way of relationship with the Lord — the things to which we are especially sensitive and often fearful.

R. called this morning to ask how I was. Bless You for Your obedient children, Lord! She also gave me a section in *Transformation of the Inner Man* which was just what I needed to hear. The Lord led her to pray for me this morning. Then she called to say so.

How hard, how very hard it is to really hear and believe, Lord!

Friday night, 10-5-84

Well, I have called the pastor, and I have called the chairperson of the Pastor Parish Committee. I have appointments with the two people I talk to first in order to register my intention to resign. I believe it will be something of a shock to some, and it will probably cause a stir, perhaps more than I know. I will need a lot of talking time with people before it is announced some Sunday morning.

The amazing thing is that I am not yet struggling with the decision. I have been so completely caught up in the people and ministry at this church that up until now I could not imagine leaving or choosing to leave, especially once You told me to stay. But now, since You have said, "Now it's time to go" and have confirmed it, it is as though the heart You gave me for every situation, and for particular people especially, is being released. Anyway, already it is becoming okay with me to go. I have to say, though, Lord, that I wonder where I am going. It's a funny thing what happens when You open and close doors. Before the door opens, we can have no interest at all, and then all of a sudden You give us a heart for what is through the open door. But when You are closing the door, there is a release of heart as well and the connection gets quietly loosened as. I think that is amazing.

> *Heb. 13:14,15 For here we have no continuing city, but we seek one to come. Therefore by Him let us continually offer the sacrifice of praise to God, that is, the fruit of our lips giving thanks to His name.*

Saturday evening, 10-6-84

This next month or so is going to be an intense time. I have to go see a lot of people I care about and tell them I'm leaving. They won't have had the advance notice and preparation I have had, or at least they won't be aware of it until we talk and the Lord lights up what He has already begun. That is my chief prayer now, Lord that you prepare the hearts of people to receive what is happening.

Sunday night, 10-7-84

It certainly has been an amazing day—full of confirmations. One of the major ones was the Scripture chosen this morning. It was Is. 5:1-11 which contains the statement: "I will take down the hedge." I sat there in tears as the worship leader read it— actually during most of the service and virtually all of the Celebration Class, which I have taught for years. This is the week when only I know.

So the confirmations are numerous, but nevertheless, Lord, in my prayer time tonight and in the morning, I want to have the witness of Your own Spirit within to those things I am hearing.

Tuesday morning, 10-9-84

Underneath this agreement to leave there are a lot of feelings right near the surface. It won't be possible to bury them, and I don't want to. When I awakened this morning there was such an overall heaviness, a deep and hurtful sense of loss. It isn't of the job, I don't think, but more of the potential that got interrupted in the church. There is a loss of promise and purpose that grieves my heart; the church has lost the vitality it had a couple of years ago, and the only thing that remains workable is to go around shoring up the growth in lives that happened and shield it from being knocked out by disillusionment.

Lord, it's so sad. It grieves my heart.

Tuesday night, 10-9-84

It's only Tuesday and I've talked to a lot of people already. Your timing and provision in that continue to be amazing. The feelings about it all continue to emerge and probably will for a long time until deep down clarity and peace are restored.

Wednesday morning, 10-10-84

Lord, what do you want me to say to these people on Sunday morning? I want to honor the bond and not mar it in any way. Show me how to do that.

Thursday morning, 10-11-84

I received word this morning that there was an "emergency" meeting of the staff parish committee last night. Normally, I would be on the phone finding out, and I admit to some curiosity. And yet, it looks more like a spinning of wheels which I don't want to hear—the Lord Himself has set some things in motion. We can either enter in or thrash around, but none of us can successfully change what He is doing.

I have come to a new understanding about who I am in Christ and my relationship with the Lord and the rest of His body. I see myself bringing my piece of the puzzle and contributing it into the whole mix. Everyone brings only their piece—God puts them together and works all the pieces. There is a sense of peace and contentment in bringing the piece I have to give and trusting Him to do with it what He will. This is a gift of understanding and truth that will bless my whole life. I have never viewed myself this way before. I think it is part of the humility the Lord has been working in me and that I have been seeking. I marvel at the grace of the Lord today and feel bailed out of the heaviness I have been under and woke up in this morning.

Friday evening 10-12-84

Well Sunday is coming and I will need to address the congregation about leaving. What is the real thing I have to say to this congregation, Lord?

Thank you for helping me grow up in the Lord.

I remember the noon time today in the sanctuary. I prayed that I would be able to leave this place being a blessing to this people; You are going to see to that prayer. There will be a reception on the patio after service. I'm glad of that. There needs to be some place for saying goodbye. I thank you, Lord. Truly, You do all things well — under any circumstances!

Saturday early evening, 10-13-84

I am listening to the praise singing at the Sunday evening service. You certainly did bless us there for a time, Lord. I don't know all the things I have learned as a result of that fellowship, but they will come to light as I go.

D. called to say "I love you" and let me know she has been thinking of me and knew others were. I'm sure that's true, Lord; I feel their prayers and Your guidance.

Sunday morning, 10-14-84

This morning the sermon was on Mt. 22. As I read the Scripture I got such a simple view of what the wedding feast parable is saying. It was the Father preparing us to marry Jesus. At one point I looked out the open sanctuary doors into the sunny morning and heard the Lord ask: "Will you marry Me?" I said, "Yes, Lord, I delight to marry You!"

Monday morning, 10-15-84

It's a new day. For all intents and purposes I have resigned. There are some folks I will talk to but I am finished and the Lord seems to be saying, "move on." This morning while I was making my bed and getting started on the day, the thought clearly came to me:

> You'll have to stop listening to praise songs and get on with it.

I knew that meant the praise tape of the Sunday evening service I had been listening to for two days, and through which the Lord showed me many things. I did notice that last night and this morning it was no longer a springboard of revelation, but I continued to listen to it. This morning when I heard that it was time to get on with it, I was on my way to turn the tape over, turn it up and listen while I was getting ready. I noticed that it had developed a hitch in its get-along. It caught and had a slowing down distortion, along with clicking. So I went over and took it out, put it securely back in and turned it on—it sounded the same. It occurred to me that the heads hadn't been cleaned, so I did that. It sounded worse.

All along I kind of knew that I was being disallowed from dwelling on the past. And I asked, half-jokingly: "Lord, did You strike that poor tape?" I didn't expect any response, but I got a huge witness of the Holy Spirit. I was amazed, but that is what happened: the Lord said enough of that! Not enough of praise songs; the tape player works fine with another tape.

Tuesday morning, 10-16-84

I'm feeling more and more tired as we continue to wade through this time. Last night at the inner healing group, three people stayed home—too overwhelmed to come, perhaps. This morning I am exceedingly tired. I feel weighed down by all the sorrow and loss and the magnitude of working through it with each person directly impacted and the body as a whole. When the church is in trouble, people's faith is endangered. There is a tearing of a size I had not anticipated. I wonder how I can stand it, Lord, and I want to walk along with You without getting sick.

I want Your grace to be sufficient, but though so tired last night, I am not sleeping well — what with prayer for others and listening through for myself.

Wednesday morning, 10-17-84

Well, it's a new day. It's bright and clear today, though it rained in the night. It rained in more ways than one, as I received my prayer language last night! I was in a place of utter despair and asked the Lord what to do. He said, "praise Me." Praise?! But that is all I heard, so I began to praise, barely able to say the words and thinking what a pitiful effort it was. But I continued and it improved some, and then I lapsed into speaking in tongues and entered a whole new place of praise which made the words of praise I was listening to in a song, and could say in English, pale and lifeless by comparison. There is no telling how long I prayed and praised in a prayer language I don't understand. After I had been in praise for a while, I began to think of a number of people; as they came to mind I prayed in the Spirit and images came to mind which gave me spiritual insight into what I was praying for them. It was a wondrous time! And yet it seemed so simple and natural.

Somewhere in the midst of that in the night I heard it raining. It did not register with me then about rain being a blessing of God, but it registers powerfully this morning! You are gracious and merciful, Father.

Thursday morning, 10-18-84

I moved everything out of my office yesterday. It is still in my car, but I can be effectively finished with duties on Sunday. So yesterday may have been my last day of real duties at church, and it was my first day of having the gift of tongues, which I acquaint with a new level of surrender and need. I don't know if I got to a place of releasing what God has already given, as one doctrinal position holds; or if God chose the time and place and circumstances, which I tend to suppose. Whatever the how,

I'm delighted with the outcome. It opens a new dimension in prayer; surely there is definite purpose in the Lord doing that now.

Monday morning, 10-29-84

This is an interesting day. I am going to talk to the District Superintendent, at his suggestion. But somehow the real issue these days is not what I say to the DS; it's what I hear the Lord saying to me in terms of direction and focus. Now I embrace a settled focus on Him, out of which all things come, instead of a scattered focus on events and circumstances from which no peace flows.

We are in a new day, Lord, and I am listening!

Three

———— ∞ ————

Learning to Abide

John 15:7-9 If you abide in Me, and My words abide in you, you will ask what you desire, and it shall be done for you. By this My Father is glorified that you bear much fruit, so you will be My disciples. As the Father has loved Me, I also have loved you; abide in My love.

Wednesday morning, 11-1-84

It's a new day, a new month, and a new place in my life. Nevertheless, I'm still feeling at loose ends and a bit cut off. Leaving the position at W. Anaheim leaves a hole in my life which needs filling with the next thing, and it has to be something the Lord chooses. I haven't yet heard what that is unless it is the counseling job at CCI. And if that is the thing for me, it doesn't fit with my ordination program. I don't know what to do about that, but they can't go together.

Last night I got a sense of what the Church of His Spirit being deserted and locked might mean. The Lord was showing me that I was going to be (already am) involved in His setting free process of His children. I'm certainly up to my eyeballs in it myself! Most believers want to be content with believing. But He wants to set us free from all the bondages in our lives. There can be no church of His Spirit until that happens, no worshipping in spirit and truth. We are still in the actual activity of suppressing or holding back the truth and become so schooled in it that we think any other approach is out of control, and in fact it is — that's the point, that we relinquish our own control.

Losing control scares us away from the threshold of being set free. Dilemma!

I saw last night a link between His setting free process and the initial call I experienced the day He said: "The Church of My Spirit is deserted and locked." It seemed so huge and formidable when He said it that I found it out of the question to answer with a whole heart — I'm too small for such things, but it is surely true that He is not. It is coming into more focus these days; all the things I have seen in lives in recent years confirm His declaration and why it is the case.

Anyway, it occurs to me that the first fruits of this time need to go to the Lord. In the way I am most familiar with, I am going for a walk with Him.

Thursday morning, 11-8-84

It's 11:00 and I am somewhat frustrated at the length of time it has taken me to get going. I still haven't started on the tapes for tonight and half the day is gone.

I finally got around to praying about the question of getting involved with CCI. I thought I would pray about it, receive some confirmation, call Larry and be able to make all the other choices down the line. But when I asked the question, there was no response. It's the kind of no response I recognize as asking the wrong question, not the topic right now. So I asked what the question of the moment was.

It has to do with something the Lord brought to my attention early this morning. He called my attention to a photograph I took years ago, before I knew I knew Him. It is of a path through an orchard after the rain. The path disappears into the distance; it wasn't clear where it came out. There are no road marks, no clear destination, no guarantees. All one can see is that it goes through the middle of an orchard, which is either in the midst of fruitful harvest, or in process of producing it.

I realized that the first challenge was choosing the path, before there was any discussion of the steps down it. I held the two paths in view for a moment. The orchard path represents a way in which nothing is entirely clear; it's a path of trusting the Lord for whatever He is doing and proceeds one step at a time with Him. The other path I've been on is all marked out—you go through seminary (3 years), then apply for ordination (1 year), then you are appointed as Youth Pastor or Associate (2 years or so), then you get ordained elder and lead a church. There is a guaranteed income, benefits, retirement, and You cannot be out of a job. It's all marked out.

The Scripture that goes with the orchard path is Jesus saying he only does what He sees the Father doing. That's the nature of the path He is insisting I choose before we proceed, know it up front and choose.

Wednesday morning, 11-28-84

The time counseling last night went well. I had a difficult time getting to a point of contact with my first client, however. Finally, she said something I could get a hold of that was central for her, I hope she comes back and we can move along through that one.

And the couple coming for marriage counseling, a former pastor and his wife, went very well. Thank You for the times and the people and what you are willing to do in their lives. Yet, I came home wondering what it was all about, and what it is saying to me in terms of direction. I've not been able to feel that enthused about it. I don't understand why it is so hard for me to hear You on the topic of direction, Lord. Why is that?

You hear me; you have heard and taken each step.

Hmm…. Am I looking for a grand scenario that I am not going to get?

Monday evening, 12-10-84

Yesterday morning I was listening to some praise songs. One of them which says: "Rule over my soul" taught me something about myself. The Lord showed me a little vision as I was listening. In it I was sitting at Jesus' feet, leaning against His knees—the song was saying "rule over my soul, rule over my soul, sweet Spirit rule over my soul. My rest is complete when I sit at Your feet; sweet Spirit rule over my soul." In the vision I could see me, not so much my physical presence there, but as it were my attitude and inner state; I could see that my rest was not complete, even at the feet of Jesus. My mind was a bit agitated, in part thinking about what I needed to do next, while part of me was there in worship. I recognized that split focus, and it says that I don't know how to rest entirely. I can see that is true, sad but true.

Wednesday morning, 12-12-84

I went to bed and woke up with a dull headache. That's how I felt in spite of the fact that the sessions last night went very well. I'm especially pleased with the progress of the couple and the difference in their togetherness. They are hopeful and able to get into some of the obstacles that have thwarted that. Yet, I have one of those dull, decision, or new insight, or choice-point-at-hand headaches which I have learned to identify. I think I know what this one is. I feel pressed for a decision, and I am not comfortable with any of the implications of it. I better just look at it head on, lay out the pieces and see where You bring me. First, I am not as comfortable with CCI as Fuller in terms of its credibility in the world. A degree from Fuller speaks loudly; one from CCI doesn't say much because not many people know about it. Right now, however, it is more Christ centered. I am concerned that I will spend two years and be where I am now in terms of being able to work more productively. Or that I will have to be in the same low pay internship situation for several years after that. Then there is the fact that I feel what I am doing belongs in the church. I am interested in equipping the saints and I prefer a church over a psychological environment, though I am discovering the drawbacks of both.

There is another underlying problem, that of getting an MFCC degree and being divorced with no children. I'm having a problem with the divorce stigma. I can deal with having failed in some sense and being forgiven, but practically it sounds funny to people, and they have a right to expect that the one counseling them has been able to get it to work herself.

The other thing is that I feel some certainty that the Lord told me to go to Fuller, and to Pacific Christian College before that, and to apply for ordination in the Methodist Church. Why did he tell me to do those things if He did not mean for me to go through with any of them entirely. I have some possible answers to that, but it remains puzzling and troubling.

So I would not later question whether I should have gone to seminary or through the candidacy program, knowing by experience what they really contain.

And to broaden my understanding of the training programs and what the people who go through them receive. In none of those programs is connection with the Lord emphasized. I now know what is there and what is not there.

I am able to conclude at this point that all the school possibilities contain elements I don't buy completely. But I am amazed to find myself now considering psychology. It has some direct application in lives, sometimes more real than systems of theology have.

How can I have gone to so many schools and still have no clear vocation? Most people by now have been established in their professions for ten years and are looking forward to retirement. Why am I having such a hard time finding myself?

Because you are becoming a new creature

What are You doing with me, Lord?

Equipping you to accompany My children into fullness of life with Me. You have to go there yourself before you can be useful to them.

I first showed you what the world has to offer

Xerox

Then I showed you the best men can do on their own in the church, without acknowledging and entering into the power of the Spirit

Pacific Christian College

Then I showed you the mixture of intellect insisting on its rights and spirituality looking for a niche without offending man's intellect.

Fuller

All along I have shown you about utter dependence on Me for all things and it has served as a correcting contrast to these others.

Personal struggles

And I have shown you plainly the condition of My church and the system men have established to run the church.

Methodist candidacy

Now I will show you some deeper truths about how you and others work in mind and heart and how to use that knowledge to release and free My children.

By all these means I am building one who discerns wisely and will rightly divide the word of truth, being equipped for every good work.

Do not be afraid; I am with you to comfort and lead.

The real issue is telling people who haven't heard these things from You that I am going from Fuller and ordination to CCI and counseling. I have to acknowledge that I am uncomfortable with that, Lord. Is it my pride? I thought so.

You will be a carefully shaped vessel. I rejoice in your willingness to follow Me and in your heart to want no other path. Your preparation has been gorgeous, moving through every step by the hand of the Lord. You know this but fear to rejoice in Me. Fear not, I will be with you in all things, only be strong and very courageous.

Phil 4:11-13 Not that I speak in regard to need, for I have learned in whatever state I am, to be content. I know how to be abased, and I know how to abound. Everywhere and in all things I have learned both to be full and to be hungry, both to abound and to suffer need. I can do all things through Christ who strengthens me.

Saturday 12-15-84

There is a new quality to the day. I don't know why I would be changing schools again, but I am coming to peace with it. It bears on the preparation God is working in me and on the gradual wearing away of attitudes that have not allowed me to receive what He is doing without complaint. It has taken a long time for my expectations and view of me to change enough to accept the vessel You are making me into, Lord. It all depends on how seriously we want to take You.

Monday evening, 12-17-84

I have some appointments tomorrow night, and this group on Thursday night. I need to get well, but I believe this cold is related to whatever issue I'm being pressed to grow through at this point. It seems to center on choosing to follow Jesus, not worrying about credentials, or job, or money, or outcome, or if anything I am doing is going anywhere at all. I had looked forward to being a minister. Now it seems I get to minister intensely but not have that position in the church. Somehow I am having a hard time letting go of that. It is what my family and friends have been expecting, and I kind of liked the idea too, but I had a misconception of how it works in reality. Apparently I am being shaped into a different sort of vessel, and it doth not yet appear what that will be. In my heart I'm arguing with you, aren't I, Lord? And it's got to stop? That's what I thought. So how do I let go of my expectations and enter into Your plan, Lord?

Praise, giving thanks for all things, in all things. Worship.

This long trail of healing and all the missed opportunities and destructiveness of my wounds, how can I thank You for all that, Lord?

> You have been given many gifts and graces, along with intelligence. What do you think you would have done with them had you been free to join all the possible places where they could be spent? I can only restore and heal as My children come in known need. You would not have needed Me apart from that deep wound and the isolation it caused. Praise God for protecting you until in the fullness of time He brought about your restoration and redeeming of the years now in progress.

> You have the ability to be successful in your own right, if you could have tolerated living in the midst of others doing the same. Look at D; he has many of the same gifts, but is less wounded in his person. Nothing he does is for My glory. We have no fellowship together; he is sufficient unto himself. Which would you prefer?

Monday morning, 2-11-85

Since attending the women in ministry conference last week, I have spent every available minute in the word. The Lord is opening Scripture to me, and I am either rejoicing in realizations about Him, or I am convicted and repenting of realizations about me. *Eph. 1* gave me some exciting revelation of Jesus Christ, and I had to confess to the Lord again that I have such a small view of Him, but I could rejoice in it being expanded as I read.

Then I read *Col. 3* which has equal depth of revelation, but it's about me, about God's children, about our nature, not His. There was conviction right and left, mostly over a certain rebellion toward taking Him really seriously in stripping away the things that cannot agree or comply. And in Rom. 12, which

I just read, it says, "in honor preferring one another." I could feel resistance in my heart over that, not being willing to prefer some over me.

One of the other things that stood out was Paul's willingness in *Col. 1* to "fill up that which is behind of the afflictions of Christ in my flesh for His body's sake, which is the church." Yes, God loves His church and wants to see it fully reconciled to Himself. I don't think my attitude toward the church is fully reconciled, but it does have to do with us not being fully reconciled and the mess that makes.

Monday evening 2-11-85

I'm beginning to read through Romans. Verse 1 says Paul is a servant of Jesus Christ, called to be an apostle, and then it says, "separated unto the gospel of God." Separated means to set off by boundary, i.e., limit, exclude, appoint, divide, sever. I can relate to all those words of definition; they are going on in my life. I have been excluded from some things as I continue to choose Christ; appointed to certain works; divided from some places I used to be, severed literally. The question is whether it is God doing the separating, which I am okay with, or me doing it, which would be disastrous. How to tell which is which is a maturing challenge of the first magnitude!

> *Rom. 1:10,11 making request if, by some means, now at last I may find a way in the will of God to come to you. For I long to see you, that I may impart to you some spiritual gift, so that you may be established...*

I'm convicted by that Scripture. I am frequently called into a situation, but I am not "longing" to go. How do I move into that new place?

> Just what you are doing: *that He might sanctify and cleanse her"*(the church — you) *with the washing of water by the word (Eph. 5:26).*

As My word comes alive in you, it will renew your mind (*Rom. 12:3*) and you will put on the new man, which after God is created in righteousness and true holiness (*Eph. 4:23f*) Jesus only wanted to do what He saw His Father doing (*John 5:19*), so will you.

Rom. 1:12 That is, that I may be encouraged together with you, by the mutual faith both of you and me.

You do not yet understand the great blessings My other children can be to you. You see yourself more in the role of blessing them.

Hmm. That's going to take some work, Lord. You realize that their "blessing" is not always blessing? So back to verse 9 "*that without ceasing I make mention of you in my prayers.*" Lord, I don't hold Your people enough in prayer, do I? Why don't I pray for them more?

You pray mostly for yourself—your growth, your decisions, your direction, your understanding. That is all right; but you must do the other without leaving off the first. You come for yourself in order to be able to come for others, not as an end in itself.

"Without ceasing" is the key to your concern about time to do that much praying. Walk along talking to Me about these things , holding up My children, interceding for them as you go.

Lord, can I stand this? We're only on verse 12 of the first chapter!

Sunday afternoon, 2-17-85

I feel in need of a walk or something. I need to find out why I am unwilling to get involved in the Good Shepherd United Methodist Church. I cannot yet bring myself to do that, but I need to find out why. I suspect some kind of unresolved hurt or anger, and I don't want it to stand if that is the case.

Monday morning, 2-18-85

Well, I never went for my walk yesterday; and I still have questions this morning. Why do I not want to consider a position at Good Shepherd?

> Because you don't think you can be involved stating openly what you know of Me and being who you are. You fear and are made anxious by rejection or disagreement of others, and you can't bear to play the role you think will be acceptable.

That's right! That is how I feel, though I couldn't put words to it. That leaves me no place to go. How do I get out of it?

> Follow Me, take the risks, and grow through the hurts, blessed are you if you are persecuted for My sake.

I'm just not willing to share myself, am I, Lord? Why is that?

> Everyone you have gotten close to sharing yourself with has misunderstood, and that has hurt. It will again.

You know, Lord, as I write that down, I feel a real irritation and tiredness of being boxed in by that one and continuing to use it as an excuse. How can it be healed and put behind me?

> *Rom. 8:13,14 For if you live according to the flesh you will die; but if by the Spirit you put to death the deeds of the body, you will live. For as many as are led by the Spirit of God, these are sons of God.*

So the real question this morning is: what do You want to do today?

It seems that what I need is not a list I can approve and plan, but a heart attitude that is freed to follow and take the risks. That would make me free and open and responsive instead of careful and plodding and restrained. Does everyone have the problem I have with being a part of things?

> Years of isolation have complicated the coming out, but have also protected you against settling into the traditions of men. Now you are ill at ease in the midst of them. When you can be there without intimidation, the power of God will be manifest, and there will be a refined purity in the fruits of your labors. The path of learning to trust Me above all else is a difficult one, touching every portion of your inner heart, cleansing and restoring, lifting and establishing the foundations of your being—nothing short of a new creature.

Thursday afternoon, 2-21-85

I got an invitation in the mail today, to an education commission meeting at Good Shepherd UMC. Do You want me to go, Lord? Several things occur to me in terms of what they need to build things up—numbers and strength of commitment of people, that marriage film series could be helpful, small groups are a real need, some teaching on adolescence, as the gap is too great. It looks like I'm going!

I have a growing certainty that I am in the Lord's will, and that this really is a significant part of my preparation. It is me being prepared by being renewed and transformed in mind and heart. The process of uncovering attitudes and teaching me that I have little idea of my own heart condition has been a long one, but it begins now to bear fruit. There is a heightened sensitivity to when something is amiss in my peace department. Of course, we are still in the process of clearing away old hurts that disrupt peace, but one day the same activity of looking at me with the Lord will go more toward maintaining the present, than it now goes for healing the past.

So it's a new day, the sun is shining, there's a real promise of spring, trees already in bloom. The challenges have produced growth and there is much more to come. I am going to find the place in His body the Lord has for me, but it will be after I really find the place in Him He has for me.

I like writing along as You bring things to mind, Lord.

Thursday night, 5-9-85

It's quite late, and I have to get up quite early, but I want to note something about the different place I have come in ministry. I used to race around perpetually performing ministry. Now it seems I'm encouraging and equipping others as they are performing ministry.

Tuesday morning, 7-30-85

I have a deep sense of needing to seek the Lord with all my heart, to raise up before Him, into His actual presence, all that I do — to discuss it with Him, receive His mind and will and once having seen that, run with it. My spirit is willing and rejoices in that prospect. My body still complains at times, but whatever shortcomings, misunderstandings, and self-will remain, I nevertheless feel increasingly filled with His Spirit and that is a cause for rejoicing!

Four

❧

Living in Worship

Wednesday morning, 8-6-85

I was praying for pastors when I had a rather extensive vision. It was of a bridge. On one side there was a whole strong bridge. As it went along toward the other side most of the ridge had been destroyed and only a very thin strip along one edge still connected to the other side. One person picking their way across could make it. The first part was whole and strong and there were a lot of people milling around on it. It is the church, the fellowship and safety and comfort and mercy and seeming security of the church. *Gal. 6:1,2*

The point where the bridge narrows and was less populated is where refinement begins, confronting the truth about our heart and nature. It is the movement from mercy to truth. All the paths of the Lord are mercy and truth *(Ps. 25:10)* in that order. It is also the narrow way of *Mt. 7:1-5, 13,14.*

The point where it narrows over to the other side is the humbling and wisdom brought about by individual brokenness. It produces one who seeks to perform the will of God, who loves the body and will stand and suffer with Christ. *Gal. 2:19,20; 1 Pet 4:12,13; Col. 1:24*

It is the process by which we become the light of the world — *Ex. 27:20; Mt. 5:14,15.* The kind that glorifies the Father, pure light.

The other side of the bridge is communion, fellowship, or partnership with God. *John 17* being fulfilled. It is oneness, the interconnected life with God, dependence upon Him for all things, loss of self-will. The bridge crosses over to the Kingdom of God.

The following day I was prompted to ask what the whole bridge represented.

> Worship. It is the work and fruit of worship. All that is involved in that walk is what worship is. You can walk all that way and span all those places in worship of God in Jesus Christ.

> You can love and forbear others out of worship. You can face God's truth in worship. You can stand individual brokenness and be "beaten for the light" out of worship. And you can only be one with God in worship. Out of it comes all else. *John 4:23,24*

> The Scripture says God seeks those who will worship in spirit and truth. That is the bridge to God, and it spans the church, the inner prayer chamber, the brokenness of life, the sacrifice of self — all the things that go into receiving the fullness of God *(Eph. 3:19)*. Worship is the bridge for the whole walk — our attitude of worship, informed and nurtured and built up by the Holy Spirit at work in the church, within each believer.

Later in looking at the description of the vision again, I was prompted to ask two more questions. What destroyed the bridge from the point of fellowship in the church to the other shore?

> Leaven. *1 Cor. 5:6-8; Gal. 5:5-9; Mt. 16:6-12*

What is the thin strip along the side of the bridge leading over to fellowship with God in His kingdom?

> Praise. *Jer. 17:14; 33:6-9; Lu. 1:38, 46,47*

Sunday morning, 8-11-85

This is my spiritual birthday. I'm going to church on the back porch with the Lord this morning.

Saturday morning, 8-17-85

I have been reading through some journals in the last few days, spot reading. But it has occurred to me that last year was an important time, and I need a better perspective on it before we go on from here.

I was thinking yesterday about what I would do in Wrightwood on this week's vacation coming up. I don't feel pressed or confused or exhausted as I have been on other breaks. Last night it occurred to me to excerpt the significant passages from last year and group them together. I know God did some amazing things, but I have not taken enough time with them to take them in fully. So it looks like I'll be taking my typewriter up to Wrightwood and spending the week putting journal entries together, in between walks and relaxation.

I went to bed last night aware that God has answered my questions and need for clarification wonderfully. But I have taken up the answers lightly and moved slowly in them. I was asking the Lord about that when I went to bed. This morning it was still on my mind and I got an answer. Our hearts (inner personal lives) are hardened, even to God, and we need the foreskins circumcised, as it says in *Jer. 4*. He's not talking to the heathen when He says that, but to His own people. Who is so blind as My servant, He says in Isaiah. It's true, Lord, I really need my heart softened and the protective covering(s) removed. I guess we've been doing that—at a merciful pace.

Monday night, 8-19-85

I got a call from Good Shepherd UMC tonight. They have gotten an interview committee together for Thursday night at 7:00. So they are going to do it before I go on vacation. Interesting. I had assumed it would be after I got back. The Thursday night group meets at that same time. They will be praying as the meeting proceeds.

Monday afternoon, 8-24-85

Here I am in Wrightwood. I arrived a couple of hours ago. I have unpacked, gone to the store, had some lunch. Now I am having my first cup of tea and launching into a new journal. I have a lot of mixed feelings about being here and staying for the week.

I had an interesting thought picture on the drive up. I had a thought of my heart—physical heart sort of, covered over with a thick, leathery skin, hardened, I suppose. It has been thinned down to a little crust and that was all that still covered my heart. It was thinner than an egg shell. Then I thought that removing all the other thicknesses or layers which had taken a lot longer and was more difficult. Yet this thin crust, which would take practically nothing to remove, would be more painful because it would expose my heart completely. For a little instant I felt the vulnerability of that, and the entry I wrote September 14 last year came to mind—the almost physical pain I felt in loving some people and praying for them.

It was a thought related to why I'm here, to have that thin layer removed. Hmm…. I can both rejoice in that thought and wince at the very thought of it. But I can't say I haven't been warned.

I had intended to bring a favorite mug but forgot. I'll take a walk to and around town and find myself a mug. It's a beautiful day.

I'm back, with a neat new mug and a suggestion—start with a Bible Study. The Scripture that occurred to me was the place in *Jer. 4* where it talks about circumcising our heart.

> *Jer. 4:3,4 Break up your fallow ground, and do not sow among thorns.*

> *Circumcise yourselves to the Lord, and take away the fore-*
> *skins of your hearts.*

Break up the untilled ground and do not try to plant among thorns. Circumcise your hearts so nothing is between you and the Lord.

Another Scripture that came to mind is

> Is. 11:3f *His delight is in the fear of the Lord,*
> *And He shall not judge by the sight of His eyes,*
> *Nor decide by the hearing of His ears;*
> *But with righteousness shall He judge the poor,*
> *And decide with equity for the meek of the earth…*

Even Jesus did not judge by what He saw or heard. It says to me do not trust in or judge by your own faculties. They are far less trustworthy than His. That means a complete dependence on God for His perspective and being more bent on knowing it and joining Him in it than devising my own.

Father, I agree with You and I dimly see, but I have no understanding of how to actually do that. I really don't even know how I feel about it entirely. But I guess that is what we are doing here this week.

> Deut. 30:6 *And the Lord your God will circumcise your*
> *heart and the heart of your descendants, to love the Lord*
> *your God with all your heart and with all your soul, that*
> *you may live.*

Only way it can happen, I'm sure. You are the one who knows what that means and when it is accomplished. But here I am, Lord, blind and thick as I am, here I am.

Tuesday morning, 8-27-85

It is a lovely, cool morning, and I feel better. This morning I am going to begin typing what I heard from the Lord last year. In thinking about that I remembered something Iverna Tompkins said: "Everything depends upon what you do with what God says."

Tuesday night, 8-27-85

I spent much of the day typing and got through the first journal. The next one spans the time leading up to the Lord saying now it is time to go, to leave W. Anaheim. I am feeling a little at loose ends tonight. It is an odd vacation. I don't know the purpose of doing this, and I have made less progress than I thought. There are eight journals; I have only typed one, read through one more and may finish a third tomorrow, if I work hard. What is this all about, Lord? Why am I doing this?

I think I will find the point of agreement I have avoided, going through the journals will uncover and remind me. But it is a lot of work. And it's an odd vacation, which apparently does not trouble the Lord.

Wednesday morning, 8-28-85

I saw something in *1 Thessalonians* last night. Verse 1:4 says, "knowing, brethren beloved, your election to God." Paul recognizes that those brothers and sisters God has given him to work with are God's elect. In that I heard an exhortation, the Lord wants me to take Him seriously — they and I really are God's elect and I need to see that and treat me and them as such.

I begin to see, Lord, what all of my friends have been trying to tell me, and what You have been showing me for years. It's the healing you told me I came for, and it's what these years have been all about — "and have not love, I am nothing."

When it's finally visible to my deep heart, it is simple. It is the only thing that really liberates people. It is what we have all been wounded from lack of; it is the crux of our separation from God — God is love. There is no meaningful ministry without it, but our hearts have to be broken into and tolerate staying that way in order to live there.

I went for a walk through and past town. On the way the sun was behind me; it was very cool and fresh. On the return I was facing the morning sun directly. I thought/heard: "The walk back will be much brighter." I knew it did not mean the walk back to the cabin, but home because of some outcome I was in the midst of receiving.

I'm ready to begin my typing task again. Too bad my writing is so illegible; I'd just need a copier. No, the whole labor is profitable for correction and instruction,

Wednesday night, 8-28-85

Well, I've been typing all day, except for a couple of walks. I'm feeling completely saturated at this point, and I have only finished going through three journals. There are five to go. It looks like a hopeless task to record for posterity or personal clarification the things God has said. It is a fairly constant flow, so what am I doing, Lord? The only reason I have is a sense of certainty that You told me to do this.

I won't be doing any more typing tonight. I finished the third journal a while ago, and I will read through the fourth. Then I will be ready to start typing the excerpts in the morning. However, tomorrow is my last full day here; I cannot finish what I brought.

One thing is clear: the relationship with the Lord these journals indicate is an amazing thing; and the view they give of His means of preparing His children is too. I think they reflect that more than anything else.

Thursday morning, 8-29-85

In the journal I read last night there isn't much to type. The times during which I am having a choice tested and tried and arguing with God about it net very little truth, other than that which testifies to our sin nature and unyielding hearts. I had ample witness to that in the December-February journal.

Thursday night

I have finished all the typing I am going to do this trip. I went through five journals. I read through, corrected typing errors, noted how bizarre my experience with God might be thought by some, packed up the journals and they are ready to take home. But the question of what I am going to do with this legible version is not yet answered.

Friday morning, 8-30-85

Here it is Friday. Several things have happened this vacation week. The first has to do with these journal entries, what I have done to chronicle God's preparatory work in my life. There aren't so many views of that around. The Lord's preparation of His children, being so personal and deep heart oriented is done under cover. People struggle through it not knowing whether to trust their experience of God. The truth is that when they are released from school and no longer monitored, it will be the chief and most trustworthy thing they will have. I think it is not made more explicit because it is always tremendously personal, dealing with those deep places in our soul we would not choose to make public. In that sense it has aspects of therapy. It has been my therapy. But the other aspect which therapy cannot touch is the gathering into God's bosom, settled in our life belonging to Him and best orchestrated by Him—"that in everything ye are enriched by Him, in all utterance, and in all knowledge" *(1 Cor. 1:5 KJV).*

The issue is one of witnessing to that reality and opening a door for its flow in lives. I believe I am in some way going to more publicly witness to that critical preparation of lives and help my brothers and sisters have the courage to take it up and encourage one another to live there.

A Scripture that has come to mind numerous times this week and has come up in places over the years, always scaring me, is

> *Mt. 10:27 Whatever I tell you in the darkness, speak in the light; and whatever you hear in the ear, preach on the housetops.*

That Scripture is surrounded on both sides—coming and going—with admonitions to "fear not them." That's the barrier all right.

The second thing is about having my heart circumcised and keeping it open. Open to the hurt and pain of others and to my own, but it will also be to the amazing love of God shed abroad to an open heart. I could see that last night in my prayer for people. I began praying from knowledge and the distance which coming from the head maintains. But when I asked God to help me pray, He gave me insight into how they felt and what it was like for them, their fear and anxiety, and I prayed for them from the heart, touched by compassion and probably sharing the Lord's.

I noticed a real pattern as I went through the journals. When God is bringing together a new thing, it is attended by consistent revelation, many confirming incidents, visions, prayer assurance, as well as outcomes in the body—events. And the experience with God is rich and amazing. Then comes the time of testing and establishing what He birthed and there is thrashing and turmoil. During those times there is little worth excerpting from my journals, but it produces reconciled agreement at last. Then begins again the rich outpouring of word and fellowship and the next impartation is birthed. It is a pattern I could see clearly. All the argument parts then look silly, but they were real and necessary at the time. Those feelings are there, and the Lord does not bypass them. He triggers and uncovers them so they can be discarded or exchanged under a bright light which reveals what they are.

This week has helped me take a giant step toward being reconciled to what God's hand of preparation has been in my life. I have argued with it all along. This morning I have a sense of profound agreement and gratefulness. We aren't worth much in the kingdom of God if we take our orders from a variety of places and indulge our body in comfortable places. There is no easy way to show us that is what we are doing. It has to be tested and tried and lit up as it bumps into God's word and directives. It is what we do when that happens and what we choose that indicates in whose kingdom we are living. And we have to be shown that much of the time we are living in our own kingdom and trying to find the right key to get God to agree with it and add His powerful resources to make it work. That's a painful and time-consuming process for which there seems to be no equivalent.

Until He has done His own preparation of our hearts and the relationship with Him is constant, we cannot see or tolerate the first thing a new heart asks of its Father:

Thy kingdom come.

It has been a challenging week, Lord. I'm grateful to You for the courage to come and for the incredible way You have held my life together for me so You could give it back to me.

Now it's time to go back down the mountain.

Conclusion

Less than two years after these last entries, I was given a non-profit corporation. There for a number of years I was able to investigate the implications of the way the Lord heals us and develop counseling and teaching ministries that depend on His active involvement. His healing happens by reconciling all things to Himself — a series of reconciling exchanges, which He described in *Is. 61*. Of course, whatever is reconciled is made whole.

There are several bright pictures of this need for reconciliation, which He announced, led His disciples through, and laid out clearly for us to understand with the Help of the Holy Spirit. When Jesus began to preach, He said that the kingdom of God had drawn near, was at hand. Therefore repent (reconsider, think differently) and believe the good news that the kingdom is at hand (*Mark 1:15*). Believe Him instead of all the other things we've learned to believe from lesser sources — reconcile your heart with His. He knew very well how many things we have to reconsider and what a process that would be. I doubt that anyone realized the full implication of what He was saying when He began to preach. He started to address our condition anyway, until we could hear.

Then He announced that He came to heal the broken-hearted. Brokenness of the center of our being is a serious condition, caused by things lodged there that are neither true nor life-giving. We all have a fairly large number of those to clear and cleanse and silence. A certain amount of clearing has to happen to restore enough connection with Him for the reconsidering process to proceed; it has to make it through all the elements that call for purifying. The reconsidering has to happen with

Him, however; it's no good reconsidering using our own logic and knowledge base.

In those years of investigation I went through the aspects of the Fall of man and discovered how much we still operate in the attitudes that block connection, hearing, and following. Those elements bear great responsibility for the wrong things we have learned, which rise up to argue with the Lord about His ways. In that new environment the Lord gave me, I depended more deeply on the Lord to wade into the labyrinth of hearts, trusting Him to bring about truth and freeing, which He has been faithful to do. In that process I discovered how many people want their healing to proceed WITH the Lord, how many are looking for deeper connection and confused about what gets in the way of it.

Several years ago I wrote a book about what I discovered in that research laboratory. It was an attempt to lay out in order the things that block fellowship and abiding with the Lord, and the means for lifting and removing them so the way can be cleared for union. The book is called, *Seek Me and Find Me*, a much more in depth look at things than I am summarizing here. A revised version of Chapter 9 from that book is now the Appendix to this book because it encapsulates the Lord's means of healing and bases it on scriptural authority.

In the 1984, 1985 journal entries about preparation, I had no idea that I was headed toward the outcome that has occurred, but the outcome only makes sense in light of the whole journey. Working with children in the church, with two youth groups, with adult ministry, with small groups and individual counseling sessions — they all were both refining me and teaching me about the condition of man at all ages and how the Lord means to gather His children — He is immensely thorough!. He was first preparing my heart and applying to me what I would learn to accompany others through to their healing with Him. Then He arranged a little enclave where that kind of healing could be grasped, developed, and proceed for whoever was interested in that approach. It says to me now that the confusing parts are headed somewhere. It takes longer to get there than we would like, but if we will stay tuned with the Lord, He will bring about His purposes. I'm not implying that coming to grasp His purpose is automatic. I believe it is contingent on continued listening, or resumed listening.

But sometimes someone else's story may help us make sense of our own because we are one body, all making our way through confusing territory to the place and work He designed for us. Wherever you are on your journey with God, I wish you well and God speed.

Appendix

Isaiah 61:1-3

Isaiah 61 prophetically announces several broad intents of the Lord: the restoration of Israel; the coming of Jesus; and healing the broken hearted. What it says about healing broken hearts, contingent upon the gospel, applies to the whole human race, should they choose to respond to His offer. Healing broken hearts and restoring people is remarkably the same for Jew or Gentile, or indeed any human being.

> *Rom. 10:12 For there is no distinction between Jew and Greek, for the same Lord over all is rich to all who call upon Him.*

My intent is to lay out the biblical progression for healing, how it is *applied by the Lord*, and the outcome for those who participate in it with Him. *Luke 4:18* reports that Jesus took the scroll of *Isaiah 61* and read from it:

> *Is. 61:1* (KJV) *The Spirit of the Lord is upon me, because he hath anointed me to preach the gospel to the poor; he hath sent me to heal (bind up) the brokenhearted, to preach deliverance to the captives, and recovering of sight to the blind, to set at liberty them that are bruised.*

The order of what He says is as significant as the heart condition He identifies. The first priority is to preach the good news to the poor, that is, the meek and humble, either in attitude or circumstance or both. Wilson defines poor as the "oppressed, afflicted, wretched, but everywhere with the accessory idea of humility." To preach good news to the ones who need to know that God sees and cares about them, and who are in a humble enough condition to hear—e.g., the fishermen responded more readily than the Pharisees. Humility calls for honest awareness of our condition—brokenhearted, captive, blind to certain critical truths, and needing to be set free from what has oppressed our lives. In one verse Isaiah and Luke are describing the condition of man since the Fall, declaring not only our brokenness but four stages the Lord intends to lead us through to recovery. Those stages of recovery stand out better in the KJV, and I have therefore chosen to use it for this passage.

Stage One

The phrase in *Is. 61* for heal the brokenhearted is "bind up" the broken hearted. The word heal, sometimes used in translation, is not referenced in Strong's; it is the word bind or bind up that we must look to for definition of the nature of the first stage of recovery. It means to wrap tightly, as in swaddling, but this is a swaddling of the heart or we could say of the soul. Remember what brokenhearted means from Chapter 7; the word is *shabar*. It means to burst, crush, and destroy, to break down, off, or in pieces— a rather severe breaking. There are two primary implications to binding up our heart: one is like medically tending to torn or crushed flesh; the other is what tending communicates emotionally and spiritually and how it restores connection, security, and hope.

The first thing the Lord would impart is the quality of His love, likened to wrapping tightly or swaddling. That kind of wrapping brings an experience of being treasured, already a healing message. It is potentially wordless; a simple and powerful gesture which imparts safety, security, and comfort—these are the initial priorities. Comfort feels like binding up the wound; it communicates that brokenness matters, that someone gets it, cares, starts to intervene in a harmless, non-scary, assuring way that brings hope and begins to apply what needed to happen when the breaking occurred but was unavailable then. I have seen this kind of response from the Lord many times; it is characteristic of His initial encounters with His children. He does not start with things that greatly challenge us but makes a way for comfort, acceptance, and safety to register. He shows us the tender side of His nature first — not that there isn't a stern, truth-oriented side, but the Scripture often speaks of mercy and truth, in that order — mercy comes first.

When the love and compassion of the Lord settle upon someone, people who may have been anxious and relatively alone all their lives often say: I feel so peaceful. It's because they have been joined. The root word for peace means to join; to set at one again. Stage One is to be wrapped tightly in His love, to experience being cared about simply, profoundly, and in a way that works to dispel shame and fear. That experience with the Lord is usually accompanied by tears, though the person wouldn't be quite able to explain them; it's being touched so tenderly and lovingly that tears are the only response that matches.

Experiencing the Lord wrapping us in His love brings peace and security. Then we can see how different it is from what has happened in the past, and realize that He does not advocate or agree with the breaking influences imparted to us and does not go about connection the way people did who weren't listening to Him. Stage One calls for frequent repetition, as do all the stages — they are meant to be ongoing resources for transacting life with the Lord. This is especially true at critical junctures when security and turning to the Lord for truth are needed. These interactions serve to open the door to the second stage.

Stage Two

With security and a place of refuge established, we are better able to hear Him preach deliverance to the captives. Deliverance from captivity speaks to the multi-faceted spiritual battle that has diverted us from God and holds us captive. There is an implied reference to delivering us from the deceit that disconnected us in the garden and has produced endless complications since. The meaning of the word captive says as much. It means a prisoner of war. Who is the war between? Primarily good and evil, God and the serpent, who deceitfully abducted us in such a way that we didn't know we were being abducted. In this stage we begin to realize that many of the things we have taken in as truth are not true; they didn't come from the Lord, and they do not agree with Him. They in fact hold us in an illegitimate bondage which we have not been able to see clearly and therefore do not know that it is bondage and can be broken. This is true whether the bondage is by direct assault and deliberate plantings of the enemy, or it comes through the common blindness of man since the Fall. More often than not it is a mysterious combination of both, which makes it devilishly difficult to track! Stage Two means to take apart the false structures and their imprisoning influences and to replace them with the Creator's view and provision for the life He gave.

Stage Three

As spiritual awareness and discernment grow in Stage Two, it leads to the development of Stage Three—recovery of sight to the blind. Blind is a word with huge scope. It means the physically blind, many of whom the Lord healed. I love Bartimaeus, there beside the road yelling out to Jesus because he knows He is passing in front of him. Jesus stops and asks him what he wants, and Bartimaeus says: that I might have my sight. There is no greater difference to be made in Bartimaeus' life than that! And Jesus does restore his physical sight. But blind also refers to metaphorical sight, dulling of intellect or spiritual perception—blind to the things of God. A good description of metaphorical blindness is given in *Is 42: 16; 18-20*

> *I will bring the blind by a way they did not know;*
> *I will lead them in paths they have not known.*
> *I will make darkness light before them,*
> *And crooked places straight,*
> *These things I will do for them,*
> *And not forsake them.*

Hear, you deaf;
And look, you blind, that you may see.
Who is blind but My servant,
Or deaf as the messenger whom I sent?
Who is blind as he who is perfect,
And blind as the Lord's servant?
Seeing many things, but you do not observe;
Opening the ears, but he does not hear.

Obviously we all fit somewhere into that description because we are prone to think we know and to count ourselves among those who aren't blind, when many things are not yet reconciled or exchanged for the Lord's light. When Jesus was talking about spiritual blindness in *John 9:39f*, the Pharisees were offended: Surely, You are not calling us blind. His response ties their pride to sin (knowing better than God):

> *Jesus said to them, "If you were blind, you would have no sin; but now you say, 'We see.' Therefore your sin remains."*

Stage Three is an ongoing part of healing, one we can expect to have continue throughout life, as there is no way to exhaust the things the Lord is teaching us and moving us into with Him. But it must start with and be pursued from the perspective that indeed there are areas of blindness for which we need recovery of sight. Humbling is obviously an element here and is a prerequisite for hearing the gospel all the way through!

Stage Four

Consistent application of all three stages to our brokenness leads gradually to Stage Four — being actually set free from the influences that have crushed and clouded our soul. When we can see, we see we are under things that have bruised and oppressed us, and we see that is not where we belong. We also begin to see that He does not intend for us to stay there! We can be freed from them and stop spinning in the confusion and frustration they have caused. The word for liberty used in *Luke 4:18* means **freedom, pardon, deliverance, forgiveness, remission**—that's the whole work of the cross coming to fulfillment, the buying of our liberty and return. The word "set" is also powerful; it means set apart, by implication those sent out, properly on a mission. The purpose for the stages of healing is to restore us to the design in which we are made, enable us to discover the hope of His calling, to be able to hear and see it, and be free to follow Him in it.

To set at liberty them that are bruised. Bruised means crushed. It is like the word for broken hearted where we began, but at Stage One, He binds us up, wraps us tightly in healing comfort and love, which need to precede the greater challenges of sorting out truth and balancing old allegiances with the Lord's central role in our lives. Here at stage four, being delivered from deceit and our sight recovering, we begin to experience release from oppression. It loses influence and power because we no longer believe the erroneous things imparted. Freed in that way puts us in a healthier condition to be sent out, no longer suffering from the bruised state in which He found us.

Jesus declares that His Father **sent** Him to heal (bind up) the brokenhearted. The word **sent** is the same word used when He declares that He will **set** at liberty them that are bruised. In both cases the meaning is **set apart, sent out on a mission**. He is sent out and means to send us. This is repeated in His priestly prayer in *John 17*; there the same word is used for Him being sent into the world as Him sending us into the world.

> *John 17:18, 19 As You* **sent** *Me into the world, I also have* **sent** *them into the world. And for their sakes I sanctify Myself, that they also may be sanctified* (purified, made holy) *by the truth.*

We can expect these stages to touch our lives continually, as they are based on *His* one diagnosis for all—brokenhearted. They are designed to proceed in order and then to overlap as various contingencies in life challenge or confuse us. We can also see these stages as His instruction and preparation for ministry — they are the means by which we are healed personally and they will be the means by which we minister healing to the hearts of others. We won't be effective until we have gone through it ourselves, and are able to join Him in how He means to deliver healing to His children. Later in *Isaiah 61* that is the model He presents. He refers to those who move through healing with Him as those who will be called trees of righteousness — people will notice the difference in them — trees He has planted who will glorify Him; and they are the ones He will use to rebuild similar ruins.

> *That they may be called trees of righteousness,*
> *The planting of the Lord, the He may be glorified.*
> *And **they** shall rebuild the old ruins…*

Once we move through the ruins ourselves, we are in a position to aid another on the same journey. It's a description of the Lord's credentialing process. He has to raise up people who know about heart healing because His whole world needs it. All are brokenhearted and all are deceived:

> *Rev. 12:9 So the great dragon was cast out, that serpent of old, called the Devil and Satan, who deceives the whole world…*

The verses following verse 1 describe how the four stages will be carried out and arrive at liberty. Let's look specifically at the exchanges that relate to the four stages, as they give a clear picture of what it will look like living through the healing stages He has devised.

> *To **comfort all who mourn**,*
> *To console those who mourn in Zion,*
> *To give them **beauty for ashes**,*
> *The **oil of joy for mourning**,*
> *The **garment of praise for the spirit of heaviness**;*

It is easy to see how comfort all who mourn relates to bind up the brokenhearted. They are very similar, but this view of Stage One adds the contingency of **mourning**—not our most comfortable activity; in fact it is something we tend to avoid. It is extremely vulnerable, and if there is no matching comfort, we will not go there. True comfort, of the sort the Lord intends, depends upon connection. We can't receive without a connection through which to receive. And apparently we don't heal without mourning and being met in it. We have to acknowledge that the losses are as significant as the Lord considers them and be met in them. Comfort is one of the most powerful healing influences in the Lord's arsenal, else mourning would simply be repeating the pain.

There is little question about whether we have things to mourn (if we just consider the ways in which we have missed God), but that does not mean we will go ahead and mourn and receive His comfort. Mourning adds an additional aspect to the binding up of Stage One and points to what binding up tends to touch as it proceeds. When we experience comfort which wasn't available when we needed it, we grieve the lack of comfort because we see that it makes all the difference and leads to deeper levels of healing.

The *New Testament* word for comfort is *parakaleo,* which is a combination of *para,* close alongside, and *kaleo,* to call—one called close alongside, who consoles, speaks tenderly to, and ministers healing. Notice how close *parakaleo* is to the word *Paraclete,* the word used for the Holy Spirit—the Comforter who dwells with and in us to reveal Jesus and carry out the restoration prophesied. Comfort is relational, deeply relational, whereas most of our means of compensating for the lack of it aren't relational— food, alcohol, drugs, shopping, gambling, etc. They do not hold real comfort, so we must continue and increase them to accomplish diversion from pain—the best they can do.

When the reality hits that things occurred that have caused brokenness, comfort enables us to let go of its devastating effects, *in exchange* for being valued, heard, cared about and put back together — bind up the brokenhearted. Comforting those who mourn is the crux of what Stage One looks like happening!

Ashes and brokenness are counterparts. Exchanging our ashes for His beauty relates to delivering the captives; captivity offers and produces mechanisms that have no life-giving power — we end up with ashes which we try to get to work. Wilson defines the word ashes as a covering of the head, a bandage with which to cover a wound or disguise oneself. Beauty refers to an adornment of splendor, to be adorned with something that gleams — the extreme opposite of ashes. If we do not have a gleaming adornment available, we must compensate with things far less effective, and until they are replaced with real splendor, it is difficult to call them a lie because we are standing on them! *Is. 44:20* says:

> *He feeds on ashes;*
> *A deceived heart has turned him aside;*
> *And he cannot deliver his soul,*
> *Nor say, "Is there not a lie in my right hand?"*

Figuratively, "right hand" refers to our strongest side. To pronounce our strongest element a lie is an overwhelming challenge, however freeing it may be once accomplished. Consequently, we remain trapped in untruths for a long time, confused and frustrated by trying to get them to work. This is the captivity described in this passage, and it is indeed formidable. In Chapter 44 Isaiah cites the snares; in Chapter 61 he proclaims how God intends to free us from them. The same word for ashes is used in both Isaiah 44:20 and Isaiah 61:3. They are ways of talking about the state of the prisoners of war, those who need their former beauty restored but cannot accomplish it themselves.

Stage Three is recovering sight to the blind, which holds some implication of mourning in that both kinds of blindness (physical or spiritual) are losses we have to mourn until sight is recovered and we can move on in life. If we go ahead and mourn with the Lord, He comforts, helps us see the truth about what we are grieving, and shows us His alternative. Seeing it in His light has the effect of lifting us out of oppression and loss. Obviously when blindness turns to sight, there is freedom and joy, exchanging the oil of joy for mourning. Mourning is truthful declaration with God. Strong's says the figurative meanings of oil are richness, anointing, fruitfulness. On the other side of mourning and in union with God, are richness of fellowship, His anointing for the things of God, and fruitfulness as we follow Him — the oil of joy is His gift of new life!

But notice that the pivotal point for these exchanges and restoration is **mourning**. It could be called the pivotal point in the chapter because it is where meeting with the Lord and His work of rebuilding begins. Well, *what* do we have to mourn? There are our own shortcomings and the cost of them. There are the wounds in life we have experienced, whether physical or verbal, and the humiliating or defiling messages that have diminished our view of ourselves and perhaps misrepresented God in our sight. There is the gradual discovery of all the ways in which we have missed the Lord and bouts of mourning and repentance as we face our sin. The sorrow over missing the Lord is magnified as we have more experience of the depth of His love. If we really face any of these squarely, grief will register, and that is where we encounter the need for the comfort He means to bring.

We have to get in touch with what we have to mourn to mourn it, else it is buried and carried as heaviness and dampening of joy. To see it as a meeting place with the Lord where the clearing of destructive heart deposits occurs is the shift in understanding needed. The Lord turns our personal mourning into greater awareness of the common condition of man, which then makes sense of everyone's wounding and moves us toward both receiving and sharing His compassion for our own pain and that of others.

Stage Four is to set at liberty them that are bruised — oppressed, afflicted. A spirit of heaviness is good at producing oppression and affliction. Heaviness is a very descriptive word. Strong's says heaviness means feeble, obscure, dark, to be weak, despondent—quite sapped of energy and life. Heaviness is the legacy of the things that have wounded, diminished, and tormented us in life. What I see happening with people as they are healed is the heaviness loosens, breaks up and gradually lifts. All of the healing of earlier stages contributes to heaviness changing. And there is a point at which we come out from under heaviness because it loses power, the elements responsible for it cease to hook our hearts because they are being broken up and replaced. There's a point at which we realize we are not so much under the customary weight of heaviness. The first response to noticing that is amazement, and then praise! The lifting of long-standing heaviness is replaced with a different garment, a garment of praise, the new covering we may not have thought possible.

In *Is. 61:1-3* four stages of healing are described; they all move toward the same outcome—setting free. The first set declares what needs to happen and in what order; the second set speaks of what it will look like being applied to us and the exchanges that are available from the saving One.

The response of those who have experienced His stages of healing is declared in verse 10:

> *I will greatly rejoice in the Lord,*
> *My soul shall be joyful in my God;*
> *For He has clothed me with the garments of salvation,*
> *He has covered me with the robe of righteousness….*

The stated purpose is healing of heart, but here in verse 10 it is linked with salvation and the Lord's robe of righteousness. It's the work of redemption, saving us out of abduction and restoring us to His heart.

Note that the healing progression happens *with* the Lord. It depends on connection with him and cannot happen without it (He cannot deliver his soul, *Isaiah 44:20*). The relational outcome of the healing He describes is a different place with Him, which was prophesied by Jeremiah.

> *Jer. 24:7 Then I will give them a heart to know Me, that I am the Lord; and they shall be My people, and I will be their God, for they shall return to Me with their whole heart.*

I think it is fair to call this a definition of biblical healing, since it is declared by the Lord and carried out by His active involvement. The individual aspects of it are referred to many places in Scripture, but here it is all together in a clear order. We don't start with being set at liberty; we start with having our heart wrapped tightly. Therefore we need to join the Lord in His order of things and proceed at His pace, first for our own healing and then in being equipped for the healing of others, should He draw us into that venture with Him. Each stage takes the time and reinforcement it takes to become established, and that implies learning to follow Him patiently, personally and on behalf of others. And, having gotten to Stage Three, recovering sight, we must realize that we might be plunged back into Stage One, the need to have our heart wrapped tightly again because of some particularly devastating occurrence in life. It will challenge us to invite Him in, go ahead and mourn with Him, and apply His means of recovery afresh.

I hear *Isaiah 61* as the heart of what God has been saying to us since the Fall: In His grace He is willing to put us back together, when He can get us to see our condition and turn toward Him with it. It's been the story throughout the scriptural record — God calling to us and us not hearing well — which continues to this day. These are the dynamics of His healing process. His stages of healing unite our hearts with His, a goal which extends far beyond easing of pain. His means cause us to know Him because healing occurs with Him, and with Him one cannot miss the tenor of His heart.

Made in the USA
Middletown, DE
26 June 2023

33651488R00054